Bodhi Light Tales
Volume ②

By Venerable Master Hsing Yun

星雲說喻 中英對照版

星雲大師 著

持戒 On Precept

Bodhi Light Tales: Volume 2 / 星雲說喻 中英對照版②
By Venerable Master Hsing Yun
星雲大師 著

Editor-in-Chief: Venerable Miao Guang
主編：妙光法師

Editorial and Translation Committee:
Fo Guang Shan Institute of Humanistic Buddhism, Center of International Affairs
英文編輯/翻譯：財團法人佛光山人間佛教研究院國際中心

Front Cover Illustrator: Venerable Dao Pu
封面繪圖：道璞法師

Illustrators: Venerable Dao Pu and Sedona Garcia
內頁繪圖：道璞法師、Sedona Garcia

Published and Distributed by: Gandha Samudra Culture Co. Ltd.
出版/發行：香海文化事業有限公司
Address: No.117, Section 3, Sanhe Road, Sanchong District, Taiwan R.O.C.
地址：241台灣新北市三重區三和路三段117號6樓
Tel 電話：+886-2-2971-6868
Fax 傳真：+886-2-2971-6577

Price 定價：NTD350（USD30）
Published 出版：May 2024/2024年 5 月
ISBN: 978-626-96782-6-6

人間佛教叢書

星雲說喻 中英對照版②

出版・發行・編製 香海文化事業有限公司

發行人 慈容法師 | 執行長 妙蘊法師 | 編輯部 賴瀅如 蔡惠琪 | 美術設計 許廣僑

香海悅讀網 https://gandhabooks.com | 電子信箱 gandha@ecp.fgs.org.tw

劃撥帳號 19110467 | 戶名 香海文化事業有限公司

登 記 證 局版北市業字第1107號

總 經 銷 時報文化出版企業股份有限公司

地址 333桃園縣龜山鄉萬壽路二段351號 | 電話 (02)2306-6842

國家圖書館出版品預行編目(CIP)資料

星雲說喻2,Bodhi Light Tales Volume 2,
星雲大師(Venerable Master Hsing Yun)作.
-- 新北市 : 香海文化事業有限公司, 2024.05
180面 ; 27.9 X 21公分
中英對照版
ISBN 978-626-96782-6-6(精裝)

224.519   113002839

f 香海文化 Q   香海悅讀網

Bodhi Light Tales

Volume ②

Stories

Biography of Venerable Master Hsing Yun

Venerable Master Hsing Yun was born in 1927 in Jiangdu, Jiangsu Province, China. At the age of 12, he was tonsured by Venerable Master Zhikai in Qixia Temple, Nanjing, with Dajue Temple in Yixing, Jiangsu, as his ancestral temple. He later became the 48th-generation lineage holder of the Linji Chan school. In 1947, he graduated from Jiaoshan Buddhist College, and also trained at various Chan, Pure Land, and Vinaya monasteries, including Jinshan, Qixia, and others. He received a comprehensive Buddhist education in the lineage, teachings, and Vinaya disciplines. Later on, the Venerable Master was invited to serve as the principal of Baita Elementary School, and also the editor-in-chief of *Raging Billows Monthly*.

In the spring of 1949, the Venerable Master arrived in Taiwan. He served as the editor-in-chief of *Human Life Magazine*, *Buddhism Today Magazine*, and *Awakening the World*.

In 1967, the Venerable Master founded the Fo Guang Shan Buddhist Order, with the Four Objectives: to propagate the Dharma through culture; to foster talents through education; to benefit society through charity; to purify people's minds through spiritual cultivation. Guided by the principles of Humanistic Buddhism, he went on to establish over three hundred temples worldwide. Additionally, he oversaw the creation of various art galleries, libraries, publishing companies, bookstores, the *Merit Times* newspaper, and the Cloud and Water Mobile Clinic. Furthermore, he established sixteen Buddhist colleges and founded three high schools and five universities, including the University of the West in the United States, Fo Guang University in Taiwan, Nanhua University in Taiwan, Nan Tien Institute in Australia, and Guang Ming College in the Philippines. Notably, he also established the Institute of Humanistic Buddhism.

In 1970, the Venerable Master established Da Ci Children's Home and the Lanyang Ren Ai Senior Citizen's Home, providing shelter and care for vulnerable young children, and elderly individuals. He also actively engaged in emergency relief efforts, contributing to the fostering of a welfare society. Then, in 1991, he founded the Buddha's Light International Association (BLIA) and was elected as the President of the World Headquarters. Under his guidance, the association's mission expanded, symbolized by the saying, "the Buddha's Light shining over three thousand realms, and the Dharma water flowing continuously through the five continents."

In 1977, the *Fo Guang Buddhist Canon*, the *Fo Guang Dictionary of Buddhism*, and the 132-volume *Selected Chinese Buddhist Texts in Modern Language* were compiled. In 2017, the *Complete Works of Venerable Master Hsing Yun* was published, comprising 365 volumes with over 30 million words. In 2023, it was supplemented to 395 volumes, exceeding 40 million words, systematically expounding the ideologies, teachings, theories, and practical outcomes of Humanistic Buddhism.

In 2023, the Venerable Master peacefully passed away, his virtuous deeds complete and fulfilled, having reached the age of ninety-seven. He was revered as the Founding Master of the Fo Guang Order, and he left behind this poignant poem:

A mind with the compassionate vow to deliver sentient beings,

A body like a boat on the Dharma ocean, unbound.

Should you ask what I have achieved in this lifetime?

Peace and happiness shine upon the five continents.

星雲大師簡介

星雲大師，江蘇江都人，一九二七年生，十二歲禮志開上人為師，祖庭江蘇宜興大覺寺，傳臨濟正宗第四十八世。一九四七年於焦山佛學院畢業，期間曾參學金山、棲霞等禪淨律學諸大叢林，歷經宗下、教下、律下等完整的佛門教育。之後應聘為白塔國小校長，主編《怒濤》月刊。

一九四九年春來臺，主編《人生雜誌》、《今日佛教》、《覺世》等佛教刊物。

一九六七年創建佛光山，樹立「以文化弘揚佛法，以教育培養人才，以慈善福利社會，以共修淨化人心」四大弘法宗旨，以「人間佛教」為宗風，先後在世界各地創建三百餘所道場，創辦多所美術館、圖書館、出版社、書局、人間福報、雲水醫院，興辦佛教學院十六所，中學三所，及西來、南華、佛光、南天、光明五所大學，及人間佛教研究院。

一九七〇年後，相繼成立「大慈育幼院」、「仁愛之家」，收容撫育無依之幼童、老人及從事急難救濟等福利社會。一九九一年成立「國際佛光會」，被推為總會會長，實踐「佛光普照三千界，法水長流五大洲」的理想。

一九七七年編纂《佛光大藏經》、《佛光大辭典》及《中國佛教經典寶藏精選白話版》等。二〇一七年出版《星雲大師全集》，共三百六十五冊，三千餘萬字，二〇二三年增補為三百九十五冊，逾四千萬字，有系統地闡述人間佛教的思想、學說、理論，以及實踐結果。

二〇二三年，大師住世緣盡，淨業圓滿，享耆壽九十七，被奉為佛光堂上第一代開山祖師，留遺偈：「心懷度眾慈悲願，身似法海不繫舟，問我一生何所求，平安幸福照五洲」。

Editor's Introduction

Bodhi Light Tales is a captivating 6-volume collection of stories focused on the Six Paramitas, narrated by the revered Venerable Master Hsing Yun. Originally published in Chinese as *Xingyun shuoyu* (星雲說喻), these Buddhist Tales by Venerable Master Hsing Yun emerged from his enlightening talks and lectures on Humanistic Buddhism. In 2019, we took the initiative to adapt these stories into English as an ongoing audiobook series for the Bodhi Light Tales Anchor Podcast channel. However, our ultimate vision has always been to present them in a book format. As the original stories were concise and lacked additional details, the English adaptations were intentionally modified from the Chinese. In essence, the English tales are not direct translations of their original Chinese counterparts. To ensure that readers of all ages, faiths, beliefs, and cultures can connect with these stories, we employed several key approaches during the transition from Chinese to English, which we will elaborate on below.

To make the main characters more relatable, we added background information such as their names, occupations, and personalities. Thorough research was conducted to maintain historical and factual accuracy. We hope this additional information will help readers delve deeper into their favorite characters and even encourage further exploration.

Additionally, we made certain adaptations to accommodate language differences. For instance, in one of the stories, one single plane mentioned

多聞知諸法

at first transformed into eleven planes, and in the end, ninety-one planes. In the English version, we changed it to nine planes as mentioned initially, later becoming nineteen planes, and finally, ninety planes. These modifications were implemented to preserve the example of homophones originally featured, ensuring comprehension for English readers.

Each tale concludes with a summary of its morals, providing readers with a clear understanding of the story's meaning and key lessons. These summaries highlight challenges people face in today's world and offer practical applications for daily life.

Additionally, we included Dharma Words from Venerable Master Hsing Yun at the end of each story, offering readers a final nugget of wisdom to take away. These quotes were carefully selected based on their relevance to the moral of each story. Venerable Master Hsing Yun originally shared these words of encouragement and advice based on his life experiences, aiming to inspire mindfulness and guide individuals in times of uncertainty.

Remember, Buddha-nature resides within all of us, regardless of whether we practice Buddhism or not. Both children and adults have the power to better themselves and positively impact the world around them. Our sincere hope is that these stories will inspire people of all ages, instilling in them a sense of inspiration, courage, and compassion. May this collection serve as a source of inspiration as you navigate through life's journey toward self-awakening!

編者序

《星雲說喻 中英對照版》，是一套引人入勝的六冊選集，收編了九十五篇由敬愛的星雲大師講說，以六度波羅蜜為主題的故事。這些故事最初收錄在《星雲說喻》，大師喜歡在演講中穿插生動有趣的故事，以傳遞人間佛教思想與實踐的精髓。

2019年，我們首次將《星雲說喻》的內容翻譯成英文有聲故事書，並於 Anchor 播客平台推出「菩提心燈」系列故事 (Bodhi Light Tales Podcast)。這些年，我們一直期待著將這些故事結集成冊，如今因緣條件具足，並以中英雙語圖書的形式呈現。為了讓來自各年齡層、宗教、信仰，以及文化的讀者皆能與故事產生共鳴，我們在精簡扼要的原文基礎上發揮想像，增添了一些原文故事沒有的情節。也就是說，這套故事書中的英文故事是經過編譯的創作，非中文的直譯對照。編譯的幾項原則要點說明如下：

首先是對故事人物的背景資訊加以補充，如：名字、所從事行業，及個性等。我們蒐集文獻和查證史料，以確保人物的歷史背景正確無誤。希望藉由建構鮮明的人物特性，能帶給

讀者更多親和力，也鼓勵讀者進一步探索喜愛的角色。

第二，根據語言差異做調整。舉例來說，其中一則故事為了彰顯信息誤導的可怕，而使用了相同字尾的構詞手法。在中文的情節裡，最初說的是一架飛機，隨後被傳成了十一架飛機，到最後演變成了九十一架飛機。而在英文版本中，我們將數字修改為九（nine）架飛機、十九（nineteen）架飛機、九十（ninety）架飛機，以保留與中文相同的特色和效果，讓英語讀者能夠充分地理解故事的含意。

第三，提綱挈領出每篇故事的主旨和寓意，讓讀者更容易把握住故事所要傳達的信息，引導省思。同時，也探討人們在現當代可能面臨的挑戰，幫助讀者連結所學，實際應用在日常生活之中。

故事結束，為每篇故事搭配一則精選「星雲法語」，作為總結故事核心寓意的智慧錦囊。「星雲法語」原是大師依據自己的人生經歷寫下的鼓勵和箴言，期望藉此帶給大家正念，在人生迷茫處作一盞指引方向的明燈。

學佛與否，佛性本自具足。無論是兒童還是成人，我們都有能力讓自己和周遭的世界變得更好、更正向。希望這套故事書能啟迪心性，讓各個年齡層的讀者在邁向自我覺醒的生命旅程中，充滿能量、勇氣和慈悲。

How to Use This Book

如何使用本書

Bodhi Light Tales by Venerable Master Hsing Yun are selected stories on the Six Paramitas: Generosity, Precept, Patience, Diligence, Meditative Concentration, and Wisdom. These short stories, in a 6-volume set, offer readers opportunities to contemplate the Buddha's teachings and concepts of Humanistic Buddhism.

星雲大師著《星雲說喻 中英對照版》收錄以六度波羅蜜為主題的精選故事：布施、持戒、忍辱、精進、禪定、般若。此系列共有6冊，讓讀者有機會透過故事思維佛陀的教義和人間佛教的理念。

Title Page 篇章頁

1. Category
one of the Six Paramitas

類別 六度波羅蜜之一

2. Story Title
in English and Chinese

中英文故事篇名

3. QR Code to Audio

a. Scan the QR code
b. Scroll down to find story title
c. Press  to listen

掃碼聽故事

a. 掃描二維碼
b. 點選故事
c. ▶ 播放與聆聽故事

01

On Precept

Keep It Secret

不可告訴別人

Bodhi Light Tales
30 Keep It Secret

Story Pages 故事內容

4. Illustration
繪圖

5. Story (in English)
English adaptation

英文故事

6. Story (in Chinese)
Original content, as told by Venerable Master Hsing Yun

中文故事

7. Vocabulary List
English keywords with Chinese definitions
to guide bilingual readers

詞彙表
英文關鍵詞彙及其中文解釋，
為雙語讀者提供輔助閱讀資源。

Scan me to listen!
掃我，聆聽故事!

Once upon a time, there was a King in India named Asoka. He was a devout[1] Buddhist. Each year, the King would attend the Sangha Offering[2] Day, a festival[3] held in all monasteries of the land. At this Festival, devotees make offerings to the monastics as a way to show their appreciation[4] for the guidance[5].

One particular year, the King decided to organize his own festival. Invitations were sent to all the elder monks of the country. The King also gathered the best chefs known, to prepare

delicious food.

As a traditional part of the festival, not only are offerings made, but a ritual ceremony paying respect to each elder monk is also held. When the King made his way down the line to pay his respects to the monks, he suddenly came upon a novice monk named Sakya. The King thought, "Who is this? I am the King, why should I pay respect to this little monk as well?" Having already paid respect to several elder monks, the King did not wish to be rude in public, so he

VOCABULARY

1. devout (adj.) 虔誠的
2. Sangha Offering (n.) 供僧
3. festival (n.) 節日
4. appreciation (n.) 感謝
5. guidance (n.) 指導；指引

從前，印度有一個信佛非常虔誠的國王，叫做「阿育王」。有一年，阿育王舉辦供僧法會，禮請全國的高僧前來接受他的供養。按照佛教的規矩，在供僧的時候，齋主不但要備辦許多佳肴美食，還必須向在座的高僧一一頂禮，以表示內心的恭敬。

當阿育王依序向高僧們頂禮時，忽然間，座上竟出現了一位小沙彌。阿育王先是一愣，心想：我是個國王，難道還要向一個小孩子頂禮嗎？可是不頂禮，又怕

- 21 -

8. Dharma Words

Quote from Venerable Master Hsing Yun
expressing the heart of each story

星雲大師法語
總結故事的核心價值和寓意

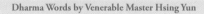

Dharma Words by Venerable Master Hsing Yun

Equality means treating others like yourself
and acting in their interests.
It means getting rid of discrimination and biased thinking.
We must tolerate others to promote harmony.
And mutual respect is the core of humanistic thought.

星雲大師法語

平等應視人如己，立場互易。
平等應泯除成見，消滅對待。
平等應尊重包容，促進和諧。
平等應建立共識，倡導文明。

01

Keep It Secret

不可告訴別人

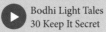

Bodhi Light Tales
30 Keep It Secret

Once upon a time, there was a King in India named Asoka. He was a devout[1] Buddhist. Each year, the King would attend the Sangha Offering[2] Day, a festival[3] held in all monasteries of the land. At this Festival, devotees make offerings to the monastics as a way to show their appreciation[4] for the guidance[5].

One particular year, the King decided to organize his own festival. Invitations were sent to all the elder monks of the country. The King also gathered the best chefs known, to prepare delicious food.

As a traditional part of the festival, not only are offerings made, but a ritual ceremony paying respect to each elder monk is also held. When the King made his way down the line to pay his respects to the monks, he suddenly came upon a novice monk named Sakya. The King thought, "Who is this? I am the King, why should I pay respect to this little monk as well?" Having already paid respect to several elder monks, the King did not wish to be rude in public, so he

VOCABULARY

1. devout (adj.) 虔誠的
2. Sangha Offering (n.) 供僧
3. festival (n.) 節日
4. appreciation (n.) 感謝
5. guidance (n.) 指導；指引

從前，印度有一個信佛非常虔誠的國王，叫做「阿育王」。有一年，阿育王舉辦供僧法會，禮請全國的高僧前來接受他的供養。按照佛教的規矩，在供僧的時候，齋主不但要備辦許多佳餚美食，還必須向在座的高僧一一頂禮，以表示內心的恭敬。

當阿育王依序向高僧們頂禮時，忽然間，座上竟出現了一位小沙彌。阿育王先是一愣，心想：我是個國王，難道還要向一個小孩子頂禮嗎？可是不頂禮，又怕

quickly signaled his ministers to bring Sakya to a private room.

The King entered the room, and, feeling obliged[6] to keep to tradition, paid respect to Sakya. Then, he said to Sakya, "I am a King and you are just a little novice monk. You must tell no one that I have just paid respect to you. Please keep it a secret."

Upon hearing the King, Sakya took out his alms bowl and put it on the table. Before the King could respond, Sakya soared[7] into the air and made his way into the bowl. Twirling[8] in the air, he swiftly[9] flew in and out of the bowl like a bird born to fly.

The King, in absolute shock, simply kept watching Sakya fly in and out of the bowl with perfect ease and wondered how the little monk possessed[10] such skills.

After Sakya landed back on the ground, he whispered to the King with a smile, "I am just a little monk, playing little tricks. You must tell no one what I showed you. Please keep it a secret."

VOCABULARY

6. obliged (adj.) 有義務的
7. soared (v.) 騰空
8. twirling (v.) 快速轉動
9. swiftly (adv.) 迅速地
10. possessed (v.) 擁有；具有

違反佛教的規矩，最後阿育王勉為其難地把小沙彌請到沒有人的地方，向他頂禮。頂禮以後，阿育王悄悄地對他說：「我是個國王，你是個小孩子，我今天向你頂禮的事情，你可不能告訴別人喔！」

小沙彌聽了阿育王的話後，就把吃飯的缽拿了出來，擺在一處。就在阿育王還沒有會意過來的時候，小沙彌已經騰空一躍，進到了缽裡；不一會兒，他又跑到了缽的外面；過一陣子，再跑到了缽的邊緣。看著小沙

This story teaches us that when dealing with others, we should treat everyone equally, no matter their age, race, gender, religion, or any other form of discrimination[11]. The King, due to his status[12] and age, looked down on the little novice monk simply because he was young.

In Buddhism, there are "four small things not to be taken lightly."

First is a single spark[13] of fire.

The Second is a single drop of water.

The third is a young prince.

And fourth, a young novice.

This is because a spark of fire can set the whole forest aflame[14]. Small droplets of water can form an ocean. A young prince, when crowned a king, becomes the ruler of a country. A young novice, when accomplished in his study and practice can become an embodiment[15] of the Truth and a great teacher.

The Buddha once said that there are two types of elders. An

彌在缽裡缽外遊走，阿育王簡直目瞪口呆。

等到小沙彌恢復身形後，小小聲地就在阿育王的耳邊說：「大王，我只是個小孩子，剛剛的演出不過是一場遊戲，你可不能告訴別人喔！」

VOCABULARY

11. discrimination (n.) 歧視；分別
12. status (n.) 地位；身分
13. spark (n.) 火花
14. aflame (adj.) 燃燒的
15. embodiment (n.) 化身；體現

elder is not only defined by age but also by the level of wisdom.

The novice monk's magical transformation[16] is a life lesson for the King not to discriminate based on age. Never judge a book by its cover. Something small and insignificant[17] today, could grow and blossom into something significant and worthy.

　　兩人「不能告訴別人」的對話，甚為幽默，卻又寓含深意。佛陀曾經說過，長老有二種，一種是年齡大的，一種是智慧高的，小沙彌的變現神異，不外是要教育阿育王，不應只有尊敬年長者，「小」也不可以輕視，星星之火可以燎原，小王子將來可以成為國王，小沙彌也可以成為法王啊！

　　總說一句，我們為人處事，應當以平等心相待，老少一如，生佛平等。

Dharma Words by Venerable Master Hsing Yun

Equality means treating others like yourself
and acting in their interests.
It means getting rid of discrimination and biased thinking.
We must tolerate others to promote harmony.
And mutual respect is the core of humanistic thought.

星雲大師法語

平等應視人如己，立場互易。
平等應泯除成見，消滅對待。
平等應尊重包容，促進和諧。
平等應建立共識，倡導文明。

02

On Precept

Dirty Basin

洗 腳 的 木 盆

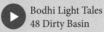 Bodhi Light Tales
48 Dirty Basin

Once upon a time, there lived a prince named Siddhartha who had a son, Rahula. Although born a prince, Siddhartha realized that in life, no one can escape old age, sickness, death, and rebirth. One day, he decided to leave the comforts of the royal palace to renounce. He was determined to go on a quest[1] seeking the answers to transcend[2] life and death. After six years of meditation, he was awakened and realized the natural laws of the universe. From then on, he was referred to as Sakyamuni Buddha or the Buddha.

After Prince Siddhartha became the Buddha, his son Rahula followed in his footsteps and became a novice monk. Rahula's teacher was Sariputra, who was known as one of the principal disciples of the Buddha, foremost in wisdom. As a teenager, Rahula still had mischievous[3] and playful habits. Also, as a teenager, such naughty habits were proving difficult to remedy[4]. Living in a rather strict environment, there were no games or amusements[5] that could keep

VOCABULARY

1. quest (n.) 探索；尋求
2. transcend (v.) 超越
3. mischievous (adj.) 愛惡作劇的；頑皮的
4. remedy (v.) 糾正；改進
5. amusements (n.) 娛樂

羅睺羅是釋迦牟尼佛未出家前所生的兒子。後來佛陀出家修道，在悟道的那一年，小小年紀的羅睺羅也跟著出家做沙彌，禮拜舍利弗尊者做師父。十多歲的小孩，仍保有孩子嬉鬧的習性，不是短時間可以改正。羅睺羅身處這樣威嚴肅靜的環境，沒有什麼遊樂和玩具可以滿足他，於是他為自己設計一種好玩的遊戲。

「請問佛陀在哪裡？」每當有人向羅睺羅詢問佛陀的去處時，他總是向來訪的客人開玩笑，佛陀明明在林

Rahula entertained[6]. So, he often came up with distractions[7] and amusement on his own.

One of his favorite games to pass the time was whenever people asked Rahula where the Buddha was, he would always take the chance to make fun of them by lying[8] to them. For example, if the Buddha was in the forest practicing, he would always say the Buddha was meditating by the river. If the Buddha was at the monastery instructing disciples, Rahula would point in the opposite direction, usually somewhere far away, and tell people that the Buddha had gone out to propagate[9] the Dharma. He took joy in seeing people going everywhere looking for the Buddha. Of course, looking in all the wrong places, they would never find the Buddha. Rahula would then laugh at them, thinking they were so silly[10]. This was how he kept himself entertained.

VOCABULARY

6. entertained (v.) 使歡樂;使娛樂
7. distractions (n.) 消遣
8. lying (v.) 說謊
9. propagate (v.) 傳播
10. silly (adj.) 愚蠢的

下經行,他偏說佛陀在水邊靜坐;佛陀在精舍為弟子們開示,他指著遠處,說佛陀到某地弘法。看著來訪的人奔東往西的找佛陀,羅睺羅開心嘲笑別人的愚笨。

佛陀知道羅睺羅說謊的行為之後,想到一個辦法來教育他。有一天佛陀要他拿盆淨水,給佛陀洗腳。洗完腳以後,佛陀就對羅睺羅說:「你把這盆水喝下去。」羅睺羅說:「洗腳的水很髒,不能給人飲用。」佛陀說:「羅睺羅,你說的話就像這一盆髒水,別人無法入

After the Buddha heard about Rahula's mischief[11], he thought of a way to teach him a lesson.

One day, the Buddha asked for Rahula to fill a basin with water so he could wash his feet.

After washing his feet, the Buddha said to him, "Rahula, take this water and drink it."

Rahula replied, "This water is dirty now after it was used to wash your feet, it's undrinkable[12]."

The Buddha then said, "Rahula, your words are as dirty as this water, no one can bear[13] to hear them."

Rahula was now afraid[14] and quickly took the basin outside and threw out the dirty water.

When he returned, the Buddha said to him, "Now, take this basin and put rice in it."

Rahula frowned[15] and replied, "The basin was just used to wash feet, it's still dirty, we cannot put food in it."

The Buddha said, "Rahula, your mind is just like this dirty basin. No matter how good the Dharma is, none of it can enter your mind."

VOCABULARY

11. mischief (n.) 惡作劇
12. undrinkable (adj.) 不可飲用的
13. bear (v.) 忍受;容忍
14. afraid (adj.) 畏懼的;害怕的
15. frowned (v.) 皺眉

耳。」羅睺羅很害怕,急忙把盆裡的水倒掉。

佛陀又對他說:「拿這個盆子去盛飯吃吧!」羅睺羅委屈地說:「洗腳的盆子很髒,不能裝乾淨的食物。」佛陀說:「羅睺羅,你就像這個髒的盆子,善美的佛法不能裝進你的內心。」羅睺羅感到無比羞愧。

佛陀對著地上的盆子,用腳一踢,盆子隨處滾動。佛陀問:「羅睺羅,你會可惜這個盆子破裂嗎?」羅睺羅說:「佛陀,這個洗腳的木盆子是很低賤的東

Rahula began to feel ashamed[16].

The Buddha looked at the basin and suddenly kicked it. The basin struck[17] the wall and broke into pieces. The Buddha then asked, "Rahula, would you treasure a broken basin?"

Rahula said, "Buddha, a basin used to wash feet is worthless[18] and is of little value. Even if it is broken, it doesn't matter."

The Buddha replied, "Your attitude is just like this basin. Your words and lies are not valued and appreciated[19] by people. No one will respect you, and no one will care for you."

Rahula, upon hearing the Buddha's teaching, burst into tears and said, "I'm sorry, I promise, I will never lie again. From now on, I will focus on my practice." After that day, Rahula diligently practiced and eventually became awakened. He was then known as the foremost among all disciples for his eagerness[20] for learning.

 This story highlights an example of how parents can teach their children. If children do not receive

西，不值多少錢，踢壞了也沒有關係！」佛陀說：「你就像這個木盆，妄言說謊，得不到別人的珍惜，也沒有人會尊敬你、在乎你。」羅睺羅聽完佛陀的話，號咷大哭，從此不再說謊，專心修道，不久成為密行第一的證果大阿羅漢。

在孩子的人格養成期間，如果沒有得到適當的教育，長大以後，說謊的習慣可能演變為詐欺、騙取別人財物的罪犯。佛陀教育羅睺羅，沒有棒喝打罵，只是用

proper education in their formative years, then the habits they have accumulated[21] will carry over into adulthood. Like in this story, Rahula's habit of lying would have continued or worsened if the Buddha hadn't taught him a lesson. The act of lying could eventually have led to criminal behavior, becoming a fraud[22] or a crook[23].

The Buddha used the analogy of the basin to teach Rahula. He did not scold or chastise[24] him. Instead, the Buddha was patient in explaining why lying is not acceptable. Though the Buddha wished to teach Rahula a lesson, he was very much aware of Rahula's dignity[25] and self-esteem. He was able to skillfully lead Rahula to recognize his bad habits and inspire him to change himself and realize his true nature.

VOCABULARY

21. accumulated (v.) 積累
22. fraud (n.) 騙子
23. crook (n.) 詐騙犯;騙子
24. chastise (v.) 斥責;懲罰
25. dignity (n.) 尊嚴

木盆作譬喻,耐心地和孩子一再說明道理,讓孩子重視自我的尊嚴,啟發孩子光明的本性。

說謊的羅睺羅,經過佛陀的感化,成為證果的阿羅漢。千年前,佛陀已為我們做了一次完美的親子教育示範,值得現代父母參考。

Dharma Words by Venerable Master Hsing Yun

Not lying is trustworthy, and trust brings wealth.
Speaking loving and tender words are compassion;
And compassion brings virtues and merits.

星雲大師法語

不說謊，就是信用，信用即財富。
講愛語，就是慈悲，慈悲即功德。

notes

03

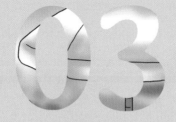

On Precept

Follow the Rules

遊戲規則

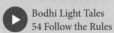 Bodhi Light Tales
54 Follow the Rules

Once upon a time, there was a young family with both children in elementary school. Due to their busy work schedules[1], the parents were unable to take their children out for short trips. However, as the children had been begging[2] about going to the beach, the parents finally decided to take them out there.

The night before, the dad gathered everyone in the living room and announced[3], "Seeing as you both have been very well-behaved[4], Mom and I have decided to take you to the beach! But before we leave tomorrow, we need to have a quick meeting, so you can both keep a few things in mind."

Slightly frustrated[5], the son, Daniel, began yelling, "Dad... why?! I thought we were going to the beach for fun! Why do you always have to set rules for us?! This is pointless, we just want to have fun and play around!"

The daughter Rosie, also shouted, "Yeah dad! Stop being so serious! We're finally going on holiday, can't we just enjoy ourselves?!"

VOCABULARY

1. schedules (n.) 日程表
2. begging (v.) 請求；懇求
3. announced (v.) 宣布
4. well-behaved (adj.) 行為端正的
5. frustrated (adj.) 沮喪的

有一戶人家，父母親準備帶領小兒小女到海邊戲水。出發前一天晚上，父親召集大家講說隔天要到海邊遊玩的注意事項，以及工作分配。只見兒子嘟著嘴說：「爸爸，好討厭！一天到晚訂什麼規則，連到海邊玩水，也要來這一套！」女兒也表示抗議：「爸爸，輕鬆一點嘛！老是要分配我們做什麼事，好不容易有這麼一個假日，何必弄得那麼嚴肅呢？」最後，這場家庭會議就在不歡喜的氣氛中草草結束。

Listening to his children, the dad was extremely disappointed and the meeting ended abruptly[6], leaving everyone gloomy[7] for the remainder of the evening.

The next day, as the family arrived at the beach, they were drawn to the beautiful sights of the golden sand and the calmness of the deep blue sea. Many people were in the water, splashing[8] each other and letting the waves wash over them. Others were building sandcastles or surfing. Seeing how much fun everyone was having, Daniel was eager[9] to get into the water. He began opening the bags they had brought with them. After searching for a while, he could not find his swimsuit. Frustrated, he complained to his dad and said, "Where is my swimsuit?"

His dad shrugged[10] and replied, "I don't know."

Daniel whined, "Why didn't you remind us to bring our swimsuits? Going to the beach is pointless if we can't swim!"

VOCABULARY

6. abruptly (adv.) 突然地
7. gloomy (adj.) 憂悶的
8. splashing (v.) 潑
9. eager (adj.) 渴望的
10. shrugged (v.) 聳肩

第二天，一家人來到海邊。望著沙灘的美好，海水的平靜，不少人在那裡游泳，兒子也想跟著他們一起下水游泳，但是翻遍了行李箱，卻怎麼也找不到泳衣，不禁抱怨起來：「爸爸，您怎麼沒有交代我們要帶泳衣出門呢？害得我們不能盡情地玩水。」

His dad said, "Son, last night I gathered[11] you all to discuss what we needed to prepare and bring for our trip. But, you didn't want to listen, thinking that it would mean more responsibility[12] and rules for you. So in the end, of course, no one remembered to pack swimsuits."

Listening in, the mom added, "This is what happens when you don't listen to your dad and me. In the end, you are the ones that suffer the consequences[13]."

As the children could not see the importance of following rules and obeying[14] their parents, the family had a disappointing time at the beach. As a result, they ended their trip early and returned home.

Soon after returning home, it was almost dinner time. Daniel and Rosie came to the dining table. However, to their surprise[15], nothing was prepared. They asked, "Mom, where is our dinner?" Their mother replied, "There is no rule that says I have to cook every meal for you! You

VOCABULARY

11. gathered (v.) 集合
12. responsibility (n.) 責任
13. consequences (n.) 後果
14. obeying (v.) 遵從；順從
15. surprise (n.) 驚訝

這時候，爸爸就說了：「兒子呀！昨天晚上的會議，原本就是要和大家商量這些事的，但是你們都不要我訂注意事項，不願意我分配工作，當然今天出門也就沒有人想起要帶泳衣了。」由於不講究分工，不重視規則，最後事情落得不能圓滿，大家也沒有玩興，提早就結束行程，回到了家裡。

can both find a way to feed yourselves."

At that moment, Daniel and Rosie finally realized why their parents had always set rules for the family.

This story highlights that many of us do not like rules, as we feel constrained[16] by them. There is a Chinese saying, "Without following rules, not even a square or a circle is possible." This means that there needs to be a set of rules or standards, otherwise, we cannot make a square or circle.

In this world, we exist and live in a society surrounded by people. Whether it be in public spaces, workplaces, or even social gatherings, we need certain conventional rules for everyone to work and live together cohesively[17]. Working in an orderly manner requires delegation[18] and cooperation to achieve common goals. However, young people today strive to be innovative[19] and different, quite often calling out for freedom without rules. They perceive these rules as confinement[20], thinking it dictates the way

VOCABULARY

16. constrained (adj.) 受約束的
17. cohesively (adv.) 凝聚力地
18. delegation (n.) 委派
19. innovative (adj.) 創新的
20. confinement (n.) 監禁；限制

回到家中不久，吃飯時間一到，兒女們紛紛來到飯桌前，只是奇怪地，飯桌上竟然空無一物，於是他們就問：「媽媽，我們的飯菜呢？」這時候，媽媽說：「沒有規定飯菜一定要由媽媽煮呀！你們自己想辦法吧！」這回，兒女們終於明白父母平日訂定規則的苦心。

they should live and work. In reality, if our freedom is aimless[21] and without boundaries[22], it can be very dangerous. Just like driving a car without brakes. As you enjoy the feeling of the speeding car, at the same time, disaster could strike any moment when you lose control of your vehicle.

Therefore, there need to be rules for everyone to follow within society, our homes, and in life, so that we can live in harmony and happiness.

In Buddhism, we are encouraged[23] to observe the Five Precepts, which are to refrain from killing, stealing, sexual misconduct, lying, and intoxicants. Many people think that upholding these Five Precepts, it is like imposing[24] restrictions[25] on themselves. However, the purpose of these Precepts is

VOCABULARY

21. aimless (adj.) 無目標的；無方向的
22. boundaries (n.) 界線
23. encouraged (v.) 鼓勵
24. imposing (v.) 強制實行；把……強加於
25. restrictions (n.) 限制

一般人都不喜歡規則，覺得受到約束，但是在這個世間上，所謂「不依規矩，不能成方圓」，在眾人集合的社會裡，就是需要有這麼一個約定俗成的法則，大家分工合作、合作分工，才有秩序。所以，現代的年輕

to help guard[26] our actions, so that we do not cause harm to others and ourselves. As a result, we can enjoy true freedom from the joys of living in peace and harmony with one another.

人，所謂「新新人類」，有些人標新立異，高喊著爭取自由，不要規則。事實上，如果自由漫無目的，那是很危險的，就像一部沒有煞車裝備的車，當你享受著飆車的快感時，也處處潛藏著危機。

　　因此，我們的社會、我們的家園、我們的人生，還是要有一個規則，大家共同遵循，才能幸福快樂。

VOCABULARY

26. guard (v.) 保護；看守

Dharma Words by Venerable Master Hsing Yun

Precepts are the jewels that adorn the body and mind.
Precepts are light breaking through the darkness.
Precepts are the rain after a drought.
Precepts are a moated castle holding off the enemy.

星雲大師法語

守持戒法如瓔珞，可以莊嚴身心。
守持戒法如明燈，可以照破痴暗。
守持戒法如甘霖，可以解除乾旱。
守持戒法如城池，可以抵擋魔外。

04

Mind Your Own Business

誰 之 過 ？

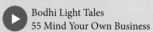

Bodhi Light Tales
55 Mind Your Own Business

Bright and early each morning, at the riverbank[1], a group of people waited to cross the river by boat. Sam, the ferryman, was in charge of sailing the boat across the river every morning.

One day, Sam overslept[2] and started work later than usual. A frequent[3] passenger greeted him, "Morning Sam!" and smiled, tapping his finger on his watch to show him that he should hurry and get ready.

To get the boat ready, Sam had to push it through sand, and into the river. While pushing the boat into the river, all manner of sea creatures[4] such as shrimp, crabs, and even fish would be pushed out of the way, and some sadly ended up crushed[5] by the boat.

Many people were waiting to cross the river, and as the boat was small, Sam had to do a few round trips. Among the people left behind after the first group had left were a scholar and a Chan Master.

Looking at the crushed sea creatures, the

一大清早，一群人在河邊等候著船夫撐船過河。等待了許久，船夫終於來到。船夫一到，首先就把渡船從沙灘上推到了河裡。可是這麼一推，河邊上的小魚、小蝦、小螃蟹都被這艘船給壓死了。

等候乘船的人很多，但是因為船小人多，船夫只能將其中一部分的人先載送過河。在留下來的人當中，有一位秀才和一位禪師。秀才看到渡船壓死魚蝦的情

scholar asked the Chan Master, "Master, did you see it? While pushing the boat into the water, the ferryman slaughtered[6] so many lives. All these little fish, shrimps, and crabs were dead. Now, whose fault[7] is it? Is it the passengers or the ferryman? In Buddhism, taking a life is an offense[8]. Who will bear the bad karma[9] resulting from this? Should it be the passenger or the ferryman?"

This is a difficult question to answer. If we say it is the fault of the ferryman, we must consider that it is for the sake of the passengers that he pushed the boat into the water. The crucial[10] detail here is that the ferryman did so with no intention of taking lives. If we say it is the fault of the passengers, we must consider that they simply wished to cross the river, and once again, in doing so had no intention of taking lives. All things being equal, then who exactly is responsible for the loss of so many lives?

VOCABULARY

6. slaughtered (v.) 殘殺
7. fault (n.) 過錯
8. offense (n.) 犯罪；罪行
9. karma (n.) 業；業報
10. crucial (adj.) 重要的

況，就問禪師：「和尚，你也看到的，剛才船夫把船推下水的時候，壓死很多的魚、蝦、螃蟹，你說這究竟是誰的罪過呢？是乘船的人的罪過，還是船夫的罪過？既然佛教說殺生是有罪過的，那麼將來這個罪業是要由乘船的人來受呢？還是由船夫來受呢？」

這個問題實在很難回答，如果說是船夫的罪過，但船夫是為了要渡人到對岸，並沒有想要殺生；如果說

The Chan Master cleverly answered, "If this is the case, then it is your fault!"

On hearing this, the scholar became very angry and replied, "Why is it my fault? I am not a ferryman and have yet to board the boat as a passenger. How could this possibly be my fault?"

To teach the scholar an invaluable[11] lesson, the Chan Master then said, "Because you didn't mind your own business!"

This story highlights that the world itself is always at peace. However, many people are nosy busybodies[12] who create unnecessary gossip. "Mind your own business" is a common saying that asks for the respect of other people's privacy. It also means that people should stop meddling[13] in what does not concern them.

In Buddhism, it states that all karma created has been initiated[14] by the mind. Our mind is the source of our actions. In Chan Buddhism, there is a concept known as "no-mind." "No-mind" refers to the absence of both aversion[15] and desire in the mind.

VOCABULARY

11. invaluable (adj.) 無價的
12. busybodies (n.) 愛管閒事的人
13. meddling (v.) 干涉
14. initiated (v.) 開始
15. aversion (n.) 厭惡；反感

While one continues to deal with difficulties as they arise in daily life and the mind, one can deal with them without craving, anger, attachment, or vexation[16]. It is important not to confuse "no-mind[17]" with a careless mind. With a mindset of "no-mind," one can be rid of illusions and discriminations, with one's mind at peace and in balance. All wrongdoings will subside[18], and one will naturally become at ease and untroubled.

In this story, the scholar's question over who is guilty of killing sea creatures is an example of the incessant[19] mental chatter in our minds. This chatter and unnecessary spread of our thoughts from a single observation pave the way to suffering. This is because our negative thoughts and emotions are triggered by external objects. Our mind is then drawn to the vicious cycle of perceptions about past, present, and future experiences gained from our senses. These senses are based on our inner urges of desire, egotism[20], and wrong views.

As the Buddha said, "The secret of health for both mind and body is not to mourn for the past, worry about the

是乘客的罪過，他們也只是為了要過河，又沒有想要殺生。如此說來，這麼多的生命喪生，究竟是誰的罪過呢？

禪師回答得很妙，他說：「說起剛才這件事，那是你的罪過！」

future or anticipate troubles, but to live in the present moment wisely and earnestly."

Mindfulness and meditation can remedy[21] this vicious cycle[22] of thoughts created by our minds. Being mindful of the present moment and observing without discrimination, we avoid negative emotions and unnecessary suffering.

秀才聽了很生氣，「怎麼會是我的罪過呢？我既不是船夫，也沒有坐上船，怎麼說是我的罪過呢？」

這時候，禪師轉而指著秀才喝斥道：「因為你多管閒事！」

世間本來沒有事，就因為有的人多管閒事，而惹出很多的是非來。一切的罪過都是由心所造，假如能無心，能滅除這許多妄想、分別，安住在無事、平等當中，一切罪過自會消滅，自然也就可以逍遙自在了。

Dharma Words by Venerable Master Hsing Yun

A deluded mind is like a hooked fish, the body and mind suffer.
A pure mind is free, shining like a full moon with clarity.

星雲大師法語

妄心妄境，如魚吞鉤，痛楚割截身心 。
真心正念，不被鉤牽，功如圓滿明月。

notes

05

On Precept

Puffin the Cat

偷吃的貓

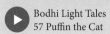 Bodhi Light Tales
57 Puffin the Cat

【家訓】
做清白貓
不可貪求

Scan me to listen!
掃我，聆聽故事!

Once upon a time, there lived a cat named Puffin. One day, as Puffin wandered around the garden, she could smell the aroma[1] of food wafting through the air. She sniffed[2] around and thought, "Yum, food... But where is it coming from?" Looking around, she continued to sniff. Eventually, she followed her nose and soon arrived at the neighbor's house. The smell of delicious food got stronger and Puffin knew she was in the right place. Quietly, seeing as no one was around, she entered the house. Puffin jumped onto the kitchen table and began to snatch[3] food. As she was about to grab more, she heard voices coming toward her and quickly escaped the house.

On her way back, Puffin realized what she had done and felt bad. She then thought of her mother who had passed away. She detoured[4] to the graveyard and sat before her mother's portrait. Feeling guilty and remorseful[5], she said, "Mother, I have done something wrong. I just stole someone's food, but it was my first

VOCABULARY

1. aroma (n.) 香氣
2. sniffed (v.) 嗅
3. snatch (v.) 搶奪
4. detoured (v.) 繞路
5. remorseful (adj.) 懊悔的

有一隻貓子偷吃鄰家的飯菜。第一次，牠覺得心裡不安，滿懷罪惡感，對著母親的遺像懺悔說：「媽媽，您從小教我要做一隻清清白白的貓子，不可以貪求人類的東西，我真該死，竟然做了這檔壞事。」牠嗚嗚地哭著，心中不斷告訴自己，不可以再當小偷了。

但是事實不然，牠又偷吃了。第二次偷吃時，牠自我安慰說：「反正飯菜那麼多，他們也吃不完，我不過是『幫忙』吃而已！」

time! I promise I won't do that again. Yes, mother, I remember your words, 'Do not hunger over things that don't belong to you.' Since I was a kitten, you always taught me not to steal and reminded me to be a pure and noble[6] cat. That's why I'm here to confess[7]. Please forgive me." Puffin cried and repeatedly said to herself, "Never will I be a thief again!"

A week went by and one afternoon, while Puffin was wandering around the garden, she again smelled delicious food. She seemed to have forgotten her earlier promise and quickly entered the house to steal again. This time, she consoled[8] herself by saying, "The family prepared too much food anyway and I was only trying to help them finish it all!"

Then, after a couple of days, Puffin showed up at the neighbor's house and stole food again for the third time, her theft now becoming a habit. This time, she sought to justify[9] her actions and thought, "Why did they leave food out there to tempt[10] me? It's not my fault!"

第三次偷吃時，牠理直氣壯地告訴自己：「誰叫他們不把飯菜收拾好，一再地引誘我上門，這不是我的錯啊！」

第四次偷吃時，牠已經像個選舉時的候選人，慷慨激昂地發表高論：「貓子的社會充滿貧富不

Without feeling guilty or sorry, she continued to steal the neighbor's food. By the fourth time, Puffin started to find her own suitable reasons for her wrongdoing[11]. She began to speak not only for herself but for cat society as a whole. She made a long and eloquent[12] argument, declaring "In cat society, it's unfair that some are rich and some are poor. There is a need to redistribute[13] social resources, and so we need a cat to carry out such duty in the name of justice. This burden[14] has fallen onto me and I was chosen."

As time went by, her theft continued for the fifth time, then sixth, and seventh, and had become her daily habit. Puffin was now sitting at the neighbor's table and eating their food like a customer in a restaurant.

Eventually, the neighbor realized what Puffin was doing. They prepared lots of food and waited for her to visit. Without fail, Puffin made her way into the house as was her habit. Except this time, she was caught red-handed[15]

VOCABULARY

11. wrongdoing (n.) 壞事
12. eloquent (adj.) 有說服力的；雄辯的
13. redistribute (v.) 重新分配
14. burden (n.) 重擔
15. caught red-handed (phr.) 當場抓住

均，需要重新分配社會資源，我就是那個執行正義的使者。」

第五次、第六次、第七次⋯⋯多次之後，貓子像個上餐館點菜的顧客，大搖大擺地跳上桌子，大口享用鄰人的飯菜。

暗路走多了，難免碰到鬼。有一天，貓子終於被巡邏的警察逮到。臨上警車時，牠對著圍觀的群眾說：「我可不是小偷，我是一個高貴的正義使者。」

by the police. And she was led, handcuffed, to the police car, she yelled to the neighbor, "I'm not a thief, I am a noble messenger of justice... I was only trying to help you..."

Despite her now difficult situation, Puffin still showed no remorse[16] for what she had done.

This story highlights how one's conscience[17] can be drowned by desire. When Puffin stole food for the first time, she felt sorry and guilty. However, this moral sense did not last long. Soon, she was overwhelmed[18] by her desires and acted in ways without conscience.

If we look at the chaos in today's society, it is due to a lack of conscience. The Buddha once said, "If one can adorn in good conscience, such is supremely solemn."

For the world to become a better place, one important principle to uphold is "humility[19]." We should have humility by being aware of things we have done wrong and resolve[20] to improve. In this story, as Puffin stole food she went through a mental process, and time after time, she tried to find reasonable

---

VOCABULARY

16. remorse (n.) 後悔；懊悔
17. conscience (n.) 良心
18. overwhelmed (v.) 淹沒；覆蓋
19. humility (n.) 慚愧
20. resolve (v.) 決定；決意

貓子第一次偷吃，心裡尚且感到羞愧難安，只是這一份良知不久就被欲望的洪流給淹沒了。

佛陀曾說：「慚恥之服，無上莊嚴。」維繫世間人倫的綱紀，就是「慚愧」。當今社會之所以亂象叢生，就是由於缺少慚愧心，如同貓子偷吃飯菜的心理過程，一次又一次地為自己所犯下的過錯，找尋合理的解釋。

explanations for her mistakes. However, she made no resolve to stop her wrongdoing.

For someone without a conscience, killing, stealing, sexual misconduct, lying, or being intoxicated[21] means nothing. If today's world has more and more such immoral people, then problems arising from pornography[22], violence, corruption, crime, and discrimination will be endless. Everyone has a personal responsibility to keep society safe and peaceful. Each of us should work to purify our hearts and minds and cultivate[23] a virtuous[24] and just conscience.

Family motto:
Be an upright cat, do not be greedy.

VOCABULARY

21. intoxicated (adj.) 喝醉的
22. pornography (n.) 色情書刊/影片
23. cultivate (v.) 培養
24. virtuous (adj.) 有品德的

　　一個沒有慚愧心的人，在他的認知裡，殺、盜、淫、妄、酒算不了什麼。但是在社會上，這樣的人一多，色情、暴力、貪汙、詐欺、傷害等等問題，也就難有止盡了。這個社會的安定，人人都有責任，讓我們一起來為人心的淨化、道德的重整、良知的挽回而努力！

Dharma Words by Venerable Master Hsing Yun

Conscience is the clothing that adorns the body and mind.
Repentance is the water that purifies the heart and mind.

星雲大師法語

慚愧如服，可以莊嚴身心。
懺悔如水，可以淨化性靈。

notes

06

Choices for Life

犯戒救人

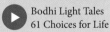
Bodhi Light Tales
61 Choices for Life

齋戒日

In ancient India, there lived a royal couple, King Prasenajit and Queen Mallika. The King loved his Queen very much and the couple got along well. Whenever the King was called away by his duties, he would miss his Queen so much that he would try to return as soon as possible. When he returned, the Queen would always joyfully[1] welcome him home.

On one such occasion[2], the King had returned to the palace a day earlier than planned, but the Queen was nowhere to be seen. He asked one of his ministers, "Where is Queen Mallika?"

"The Queen went to a Buddhist retreat[3]," replied the minister.

"How long has the Queen been gone?" the King asked.

"She has been gone for nearly a week, she will return tomorrow," the minister said.

The next day, the King ordered the royal chef to prepare a feast[4]. Filled with happiness, he patiently[5] waited for his Queen to come home.

VOCABULARY

1. joyfully (adv.) 歡喜地
2. occasion (n.) 時機
3. retreat (n.) 靜修
4. feast (n.) 宴會；佳餚
5. patiently (adv.) 耐心地

古代印度有一位波斯匿王，他的皇后，人稱「末利夫人」。國王和皇后平日感情很好，但是自從夫人皈信佛教，受持五戒以後，嚴格遵守不殺生、不偷盜、不邪淫、不妄語、不飲酒，國王的生活再也不那麼稱心如意了。

When the Queen arrived back at the palace and saw her King, she said, "Your Majesty, you're back already! I thought you were supposed to come home later today."

The King replied, "I arrived yesterday, but you weren't here to greet me."

"Oh, I'm sorry. I was in a retreat," the Queen said.

Though the King was not pleased to hear that the Queen participated[6] in a Buddhist retreat instead of welcoming him, he brought out the precious[7] jewels he had bought as gifts and offered them to her, saying, "Look what I got for you."

The Queen shook her head and said, "Your Majesty, I do not need these, please give them to someone else."

Although the King was disappointed[8] to hear the Queen's reply, he was still very much pleased to see her. He signaled[9] his ministers for the feast to begin. As the food was being served[10], the King said, "I have prepared a feast

VOCABULARY

6.   participated (v.) 參加
7.   precious (adj.) 寶貴的；珍貴的
8.   disappointed (adj.) 失望的
9.   signaled (v.) 示意
10. served (v.) 上菜

有一次，波斯匿王征戰歸來，因為對御廚準備的飯菜不滿意，大發雷霆，下了一道命令，要將廚師處死。

在過去專制的時代，所謂「君要臣死，臣不得不死」，國王要想處死廚師是很容易的事情。但是螻蟻尚且貪生，廚師也是一條命，他當然不甘願死，為了活命，便託人向皇后末利夫人求情。

for you."

As the Queen saw the many dishes laid out, she thought, "Oh no, I have just taken the precepts[11]... If I was to eat this meat and drink this wine, I would break my precepts. But, I cannot reject another of my King's gifts again..."

As the Queen was caught in her dilemma[12], a minister spoke urgently[13] to the King. The King then suddenly left the palace in a hurry, leaving the feast unfinished.

A week later, when the King returned to the palace, the Queen was, yet again, not there to welcome him.

The King thought, "What is happening to my Queen? She used to greet me whenever I returned home. But now, I'm left to entertain[14] myself upon my return..."

As it was lunchtime, the chef laid out many new dishes on the table. One of the ministers explained, "Your Majesty, these new dishes were ordered by the Queen..."

The King was now furious[15] and said with

VOCABULARY

11. precepts (n.) 戒
12. dilemma (n.) 進退兩難的局面
13. urgently (adv.) 緊急地
14. entertain (v.) 使歡樂；使娛樂
15. furious (adj.) 極其生氣的；怒不可遏的

末利夫人聽說此事，心想：該怎麼救廚師呢？最終想到了一個辦法。當他和波斯匿王見面時，就說：「大王，你回來了，我好高興！今天我要擺設酒席，陪你喝酒，表示對你的歡迎。」

anger, "Is this how she welcomes me now? With food?!" In the grip of[16] his great anger, the King immediately[17] ordered that the chef be executed[18].

In those days, the King could execute anyone who displeased[19] him. A common saying from that era[20] was, "If the king wants a minister dead, the minister must die." So, if the King wanted to execute the chef, there was little anyone could do to change his mind.

Of course, the chef did not wish to die,

VOCABULARY

16. In the grip of (phr.) 受制於……
17. immediately (adv.) 立即；馬上
18. executed (v.) 處死
19. displeased (v.) 惹火
20. era (n.) 時代；年代

波斯匿王一聽，非常高興，直說：「太好了！太好了！」但是一方面又感到疑惑，「咦？妳不是受過戒了嗎？」

末利夫人便回答：「為了迎接大王，今天破例一次不要緊！但是大王，我有一個請求，好酒要有美膳相配，我希望御廚能親手做我喜歡的菜色。」

especially for no apparent[21] reason other than the King's displeasure. So he reached out to the Queen, begging her to plead[22] his case to the King.

When she heard of what happened, the Queen thought, "Execution means killing, the taking of a life. That is against the precept I have taken. I cannot let this happen. I must save the chef... But how?" She meditated on possible solutions and eventually[23] came up with an idea.

When the King returned from another trip, the Queen was already waiting at the gates of the palace. She welcomed him joyfully and said, "Majesty, I am so pleased you are back safely at home!"

Seeing the Queen's beautiful smile, the King's heart melted[24].

The Queen continued, "We have not had a meal together for such a long time. We should celebrate with wine!"

Puzzled[25], the King asked, "With wine? What about your precepts?"

VOCABULARY

21. apparent (adj.) 明顯的
22. plead (v.) 乞求；懇求
23. eventually (adv.) 最終；終於
24. melted (v.) 融化
25. puzzled (adj.) 迷惑的；感到不解的

　　國王聽後，想到：不得了！最會做那道菜的廚師，我剛才已經下令要砍他的頭了。於是大喊：「刀下留人！刀下留人！」趕快又派人前往刑場把廚師給救回來。就這樣，御廚終得以撿回一條命。

"My precepts are important, but you are just as important to me. I want to let you know how pleased I am to see you. But... I have one request[26]," the Queen said.

Feeling extremely happy, the King answered, "My dear wife, I will give you anything you wish for."

The Queen then said, "Good wine always goes well with delicious[27] food. I wish for our chef to cook my favorite dishes."

On hearing her request, the King panicked[28],

"Oh no! The chef..." He quickly called out to his minister, "Stop the execution immediately! Release[29] the chef at once!"

Luckily, the execution had yet to take place and so the chef was saved.

The Queen then explained to her King the meaning of observing the precepts and her initial intention[30] of saving the chef. The precept of no killing means to respect life. Furthermore, the Queen was willing to break her precept of not drinking alcohol to save the

VOCABULARY

26. request (n.) 請求
27. delicious (adj.) 美味的
28. panicked (v.) 驚慌失措
29. release (v.) 釋放
30. intention (n.) 意圖

當波斯匿王知道末利夫人為了救人不惜犯戒時，深受感動，漸漸地也接觸佛教，最後成為了佛教的大護法。

所謂「戒」，是用來防非止惡，防止人做壞事的。雖然佛教講「不飲酒」戒，但是末利夫人為了救人一命，出發點是清淨、慈悲的，並不在貪圖個人的享樂，又豈能輕易地就論定她的罪過呢？

chef. Reflecting[31] on these matters, the King realized the harm he could have done. Touched and moved by the action and behavior of his Queen, the King began to learn about and practice Buddhism, eventually becoming one of its greatest exemplars.

This story highlights the true meaning of observing the precepts, which is not to infringe[32] upon or violate others. In more detail, the Five Precepts are: refraining from killing means not violating the lives of others. Refraining from stealing means not violating the property of others. Refraining from sexual misconduct means not violating the physical and mental integrity[33] of others. Refraining from lying means not violating the reputation[34] and trust of others. Refraining from intoxicants means not violating the wisdom and welfare of ourselves and others.

Precepts are like a teacher that guides us in developing a wholesome mind, body, and conduct. Precepts are like a shield[35], keeping us safe.

VOCABULARY

31. reflecting (v.) 沉思
32. infringe (v.) 侵犯
33. integrity (n.) 正直；廉正
34. reputation (n.) 名譽
35. shield (n.) 防衛物；盾

Precepts are like a textbook filled with principles, increasing our virtues so that others can feel comfortable in our company.

In this story, the Queen was willing to break the precept of no intoxicants by drinking alcohol to save a life, the chef's life. Her intention was pure and compassionate, and not for her selfish desire. Could this truly be considered as her breaking the spirit of the precepts? She seemingly broke one precept to uphold another, to preserve[36] life.

It is important to note that, no matter which religion we have faith in, we should not blindly and rigidly[37] adhere[38] to its discipline without conscious[39], mindful, and constant reflection. We must learn to be flexible and use skillful means[40] in applying the precepts in our daily lives. For example, how can we be compassionate and continue to save lives? Such is the true meaning of the precepts.

VOCABULARY

36. preserve (v.) 保護；維護
37. rigidly (adv.) 頑固地；死板地
38. adhere (v.) 依附
39. conscious (adj.) 有意識的
40. skillful means (n.) 善巧方便

所以，人不管信仰哪一個宗教，不應只拘泥於戒相，還要懂得活用戒條，能把它應用在救人救世上，能把它運用於開發內心的清淨慈悲上，才是戒律的真正意義。

Dharma Words by Venerable Master Hsing Yun

Better to observe the precepts imperfectly than to misunderstand the teachings, and thereby lose faith in them.

星雲大師法語

寧可持戒不圓滿，不可破見失道心。

07

On Precept

Filthy

誰比較髒？

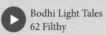 Bodhi Light Tales
62 Filthy

Once upon a time, there was a compassionate[1] Chan Master who treated all with respect and equality[2]. He had a young disciple who followed him everywhere he went.

One day, he was headed to the nearest town with this disciple. On the way, they heard someone yelling for help. They searched and followed the voice to its source[3]. It was coming from inside of a well[4].

"Hello! Is someone there? Please help me!" said the voice from the well.

The Master and his disciple quickly ran over, looked down into the well, and saw a helpless little boy stuck[5] in the dry well. Quickly, the Chan Master bent forward and reached for the boy. Luckily, the well was not very deep, and he was able to pull the boy up.

After being rescued, the boy looked at the Chan Master and said, "Thank you so much!"

The Master replied, "Are you okay? Are you hurt?"

"No, I'm okay," the boy said.

VOCABULARY

1. compassionate (adj.) 慈悲的
2. equality (n.) 平等
3. source (n.) 來源
4. well (n.) 井
5. stuck (v.) 卡住；困在

有一天，老師父帶著小徒弟外出布教弘法，走啊走地，半路上，忽然看到一個小孩子跌進臭水溝裡。於是，老師父加緊腳步，走到水溝邊，將他拉了起來。小孩救起來後，老師父又帶他在附近找到一條溪水，替他把身上的穢物清洗了。

The Master looked the boy over to see if he had any injuries[6]. Luckily, the boy only suffered[7] minor cuts and bruises[8]. The Master then said, "Let's head to the river and clean you up."

Holding the boy's hand, the Master said to his disciple, "Are you coming?"

The disciple grunted[9], "He smells! I don't want to go with him."

"All right then, you can stay here. We're leaving now!"

Though having misgivings[10] about following them, the disciple did not want to be left alone in the middle of nowhere, so he hurried after his master, yelling, "Wait! Master... I'm coming too."

When they reached the river, the disciple stood away from them, his hand covering his nose. The Master used his handkerchief and began washing away the dirt on the boy's face. He asked the boy, "What is your name?"

"My name is Ash," the boy replied.

"Ash, please tell me what happened, how

VOCABULARY

6. injuries (n.) 受傷處
7. suffered (v.) 遭受；受苦
8. bruises (n.) 瘀傷
9. grunted (v.) 嘟囔著說
10. misgivings (n.) 疑慮

在一旁的小徒弟看了，捂住鼻子，皺著眉頭說：「師父，您不必幫這個小孩清洗髒汙啦，弄得您的新衣服也骯髒了。」老師父聽了小徒弟的話之後，對徒弟說：「這小孩身上的骯髒是有限的，你的心才髒啊！」

did you end up trapped[11] in the well?"

"Um... I saw a beautiful butterfly and wanted to catch it, and then... I think I tripped[12] over a rock and fell. Next thing I knew, I was lying[13] at the bottom of the well," Ash explained.

"I see," said the Master.

Resentful[14] at the present situation, the disciple cut in and said, "Master, you're getting dirty! Stop cleaning him, he can do it himself! Your clothes are getting wet and filthy." The disciple continued to frown[15] at Ash, pinching his nose to point out how smelly and dirty he was.

The Master turned to his disciple and said, "The dirt on this boy cannot compare to the dirt in your mind!" And then continued to clean Ash.

VOCABULARY

11. trapped (v.) 受困
12. tripped (v.) 摔倒
13. lying (v.) 躺
14. resentful (adj.) 憤怒的
15. frown (v.) 皺眉

　　人身上的骯髒可以清洗，但是心裡的骯髒卻不容易洗淨，甚至身上的垢穢可以去除，但是口裡的骯髒：妄語、惡口、挑撥離間、搬是弄非、講不正當的話等等，有時候比身體的骯髒還要更加可怕。

This story highlights that though the dirt on our bodies can be washed off, the dirt in our minds is not easily washed away. Even if we cleanse our bodies of dirt on it, the filth in our speech such as lying, slandering[16], sowing discord[17], gossip, and wrong speech is far fouler[18] than the dirt on our bodies.

We should begin by cleansing our minds. A Buddhist concept urges that "a Pure Land is in a pure mind." Once our mind is pure, all will be pure. How can our minds be pure? For instance, greed and anger are the dirt staining our minds. If we can transform[19] greed into generosity, then we can bring joy to others, and our minds will no longer be stained. If we can transform our anger into compassion, then we can ennoble[20] our character, and our minds will be pure. Furthermore, if we can transform jealousy,

VOCABULARY

16. slandering (v.) 誹謗
17. discord (n.) 不和
18. fouler (adj.) 更加骯髒的
19. transform (v.) 轉換
20. ennoble (v.) 使高貴

清淨要從自己的心裡開始。所謂「心淨國土淨」，我們的心一一清淨，大地山河也會跟著清淨。心怎麼清淨呢？比方：貪欲心、瞋恨心如同我們心中的髒汙垃圾，能把貪欲心去除，轉換成喜捨心，把歡喜給人，心就不髒了；能把瞋恨的念頭去除，用慈悲心來莊嚴自己，心就清淨了；能把嫉妒、懷疑、邪見，各種煩惱、習氣都去除了，就能還給自己一個清淨心。

doubt, wrong view, defilement[21], and bad habits into something positive, then we will attain a pure mind.

Our body is like a city and our mind is like its mayor. It matters not that our bodies, clothes, and environment become dirty. What is most important is that our minds remain as clean as a whistle[22], so the rest will surely follow. What is most important is how we ensure[23] that our minds remain pure, because once our minds become tainted[24], they will be difficult to cleanse.

VOCABULARY

21. defilement (n.) 煩惱
22. as clean as a whistle (phr.) 乾淨俐落
23. ensure (v.) 確保
24. tainted (v.) 汙染

人的身體就像一座村莊，心是我們的主人。身體骯髒、衣服骯髒、環境骯髒，都還是其次，最重要的是讓我們的主人翁清清白白，讓我們的主人翁乾乾淨淨；心弄髒了，那是怎麼都無法清乾淨的。

Dharma Words by Venerable Master Hsing Yun

With an open mind, every road is wide.
With a pure mind, everywhere is the Pure Land.
For people who have joy in their minds,
every place they go delights the heart and pleases the eye.
For people who have meditative concentration in their minds,
what they hear will be poetic sounds.
For people who have the Dharma in their minds,
what they face is a world of good people and good affinity.

星雲大師法語

胸襟寬大，條條都是大路；
心意清淨，處處都是淨土。
心中有歡喜的人，到處是賞心悅目的景色；
心中有禪定的人，耳聞是八萬四千的詩偈；
心中有佛法的人，面對是善人善緣的世界。

notes

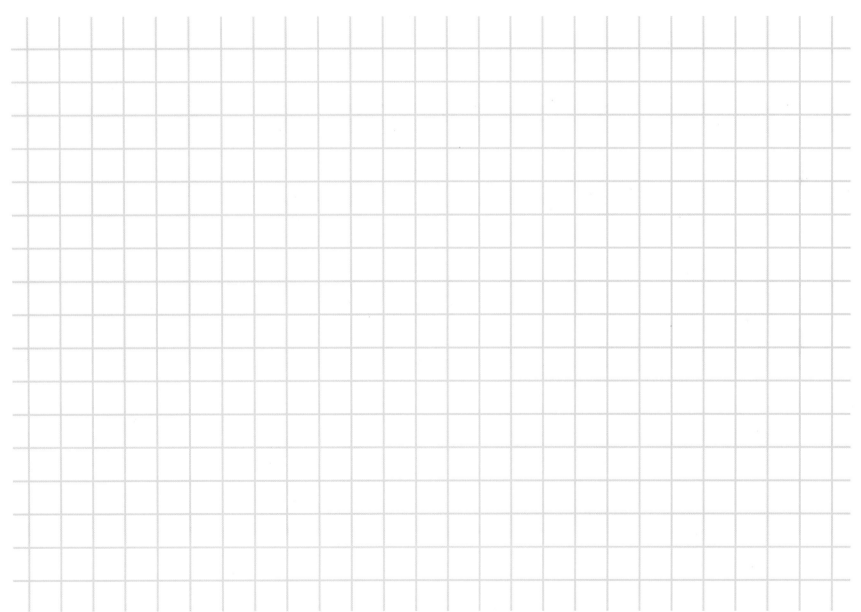

08

On Precept

No Lies

不說假話

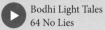
Bodhi Light Tales
64 No Lies

Once upon a time, during the Song dynasty, there lived an emperor named Huizong. He was gifted in the "Three Perfections[1]" of his time, namely, poetry, painting, and calligraphy. In those days, Huizong was among the very few who were skilled at these Three Perfections.

He was especially renowned as the creator of a font called "Slender Gold[2]." The name "Slender Gold" came from the fact that his calligraphy resembled[3] twisting golden strings. Huizong was generous with his calligraphy, often gifting his works to friends, officials, and guests.

During that period, there was an enlightened Chan Master named Daokai from the Caodong school, one of the five major schools of Chan Buddhism. The Chan practice of the Caodong school is referred to as the Silent Illumination[4], which is to "just sit and meditate" in a state of conscious[5] awareness. As a practitioner of this school, Chan Master Daokai was also known for his monastic discipline.

VOCABULARY

1. Three Perfections (n.) 三絕 (詩書畫)
2. Slender Gold (n.) 瘦金體
3. resembled (v.) 相似；類似
4. Silent Illumination (n.) 默照禪
5. conscious (adj.) 自覺的；有意識的

人經常為了自身的利益，不惜說假話欺騙別人，有時候甚至用盡心機，造謠生事，讓人吃虧、上當。謊言假話，也就是佛教所說的「妄語」，是不當的。

Emperor Huizong had always wanted to invite Chan Master Daokai to his palace, and so devised[6] a plan.

One day, while the emperor was writing his calligraphy, one of his ministers reported to him, "Your Majesty, your command[7] for Chan Master Daokai is ready."

"All right... What about the purple robe, has it been made?" the emperor asked, still focusing on his calligraphy.

"Yes, that is ready as well. We have begun preparations for the Conferment Ceremony[8] too," the minister said.

"Excellent!" The emperor said excitedly, and then asked, "Do you think Chan Master Daokai will like my calligraphy?"

"Your Majesty, your calligraphy is exceptional[9]. I am sure the Chan Master will treasure[10] it," the minister replied.

"Now, send this calligraphy along with the command. It is an order for the Chan Master to come see me. Be sure to let him know about

宋朝的時候，徽宗皇帝非常仰慕一位人在遠方，相當有名望的道楷禪師，於是就派了大臣帶著詔書去請他進京，接受御賜的紫袈裟。但是道楷禪師怎麼樣都不肯應詔。連下了三次詔書，禪師都不到，皇帝感到尊嚴受損，勃然大怒，立刻派遣大臣前去捉拿，心想：我就不相信你不來！

the Ceremony where he will receive his purple robe," the emperor instructed[11].

"Yes, your Majesty. I shall deliver these to him right away," the minister replied.

When the minister arrived at the monastery, the Chan Master was in deep meditation. The monk, who received the imperial[12] minister, asked him to wait and not to interrupt[13] the Chan Master. The minister waited patiently for half a day but was eventually asked to leave.

The next day, the minister returned. This time, he was ushered[14] to a private room where the Chan Master was preparing tea. The minister read the imperial command to the Chan Master and passed on the emperor's instructions. However, when he finished, the Chan Master said nothing, only sipping[15] his tea. The minister did not know what to do, and simply repeated, "The emperor orders you to come to see him at the palace."

The Chan Master remained silent and responded by offering the minister a cup of tea.

VOCABULARY

11. instructed (v.) 指示;命令
12. imperial (adj.) 帝王的;帝國的
13. interrupt (v.) 打斷
14. ushered (v.) 引導
15. sipping (v.) 啜飲

大臣們見皇帝如此生氣,只得聽命,拿著聖旨往赴。走呀走地,大臣們來到了道楷禪師的住處。一見面,大臣就說:「禪師啊!皇帝很仰慕您,非常誠意地要邀請您到朝中走一趟。」可是道楷禪師聽後,依然拒絕。

When he finished his tea, he was then ushered out of the monastery.

The minister had no choice but to return and inform the emperor of what happened. The emperor did not relent[16] and instructed the minister, "Send him my orders again!" This time, the emperor sent two ministers to deliver his command.

When the ministers arrived at the monastery, they were invited to the Meditation Hall[17]. The Chan Master was in deep meditation, and the two ministers dared[18] not interrupt him and sat quietly. Eventually[19], the Chan Master opened his eyes and saw the ministers. Seizing[20] this chance, they quickly presented the imperial command to the Chan Master. When they finished reading out the command, the Chan Master simply nodded, closed his eyes, and went back to meditating.

The two ministers were then asked to leave the monastery. Both were worried about facing the emperor without a reply from the Chan

VOCABULARY

16. relent (v.) 變寬容；變溫和
17. Meditation Hall (n.) 禪堂
18. dared (v.) 敢於；膽敢
19. eventually (adv.) 最終；終於
20. seizing (v.) 抓住

大臣一聽，心急了，就說：「那可不行！您不去的話，皇帝會生氣呀！」禪師說：「沒有其他辦法，我就是不到朝中去。」

Master for a second time.

After they reported on their visit, the emperor still refused[21] to give up and asked his ministers to deliver his command for a third time.

Though the command was sent three times, the Chan Master still did not respond.

The emperor, now furious[22], thought to himself, "I am the emperor! How dare he insult[23] me?"

"I cannot believe the Chan Master refuses to obey me, I am awarding him the purple robe that all monastics dream of! Yet he humiliates[24] me with his disrespect!"

Without a second thought, he sent a group of ministers back to the monastery to issue his command a final time, and ordered that should the Chan Master refuse again, just arrest him.

When the group of ministers arrived back at the monastery, one of them said, "Emperor Huizong admires you for your dedication[25] to this monastery, and sincerely invites you to his

VOCABULARY

21. refused (v.) 拒絕
22. furious (adj.) 狂怒的
23. insult (v.) 侮辱
24. humiliates (v.) 羞辱；使丟臉
25. dedication (n.) 奉獻

另一位大臣見狀，趕緊說：「老禪師，您就說自己年紀大了，身體虛弱有病，不堪千里跋涉，這也好讓我們替您稟報皇上呀！」

palace. He hopes you will accept the purple robe as a symbol of imperial honor. However, should you refuse, you will be arrested immediately."

The Chan Master remained unfazed[26] and replied, "I decline."

Another minister said anxiously[27], "Master, please… we do not wish to see this situation get worse. The emperor is already furious, and if you decline[28], we will have to arrest you."

The Chan Master replied, "I hold true to my words and vows. As a monastic, I have renounced worldly fame and recognition, why should I accept the purple robe? To accept would mean going against my principles."

Another minister said, "Master, may we humbly[29] suggest that you reply to the emperor that, due to your old age, your body is weak and sick. Therefore, it is troublesome[30] for you to travel so far to receive the purple robe. We can deliver this message to the emperor for you."

"What do you mean I am weak and sick? I am in perfect health!" the Chan Master said as

VOCABULARY

26. unfazed (adj.) 不為所動的
27. anxiously (adv.) 憂慮地
28. decline (v.) 拒絕
29. humbly (adv.) 謙遜地
30. troublesome (adj.) 麻煩的

原本這位大臣是要給道楷禪師一個台階下的，但是禪師聽後，竟然立刻從座位上站了起來，說：「沒有啊！我身體很好，沒有病。」

he walked swiftly around the hall. Though the minister had offered this suggestion[31] in good faith, the Chan Master refused to change his mind.

Determined, they pleaded[32] once more, "Please... Master, just say you are sick, and we won't have to arrest you."

The Chan Master replied sternly, "How can I tell a lie? I would rather you arrest me now than ask me to lie to the emperor. If the emperor wishes to punish me, I shall accept."

The ministers looked at each other and knew they could never convince[33] the Chan Master. They had no choice but to arrest him and send him to jail.

Soon after, the emperor learned about the Chan Master's stern[34] will that he would rather be imprisoned[35] than lie to the emperor, thus determined despite the risk of punishment and jail. Utterly impressed by the Chan Master's

VOCABULARY

31. suggestion (n.) 建議
32. pleaded (v.) 乞求；懇求
33. convince (v.) 使信服
34. stern (adj.) 堅定的；嚴厲的
35. imprisoned (v.) 關押；囚禁

大臣聽了，失望地說：「您說有病，就可以不必上朝了嘛！」不意，道楷禪師正色地說：「我怎麼可以說假話來欺騙皇上呢？我寧可受皇上的處罰，也不能欺騙皇上！」最後，這許多大臣們只得無奈地將他押解回京城了。

virtuous conduct and honesty, the emperor praised him not only for being honest but for holding firm to his true heart. Not long after, the emperor ordered that the Chan Master be set free.

In this story, the Chan Master's attitude of choosing to remain honest demonstrates that even when his life was at risk, he would rather be disadvantaged than be called a liar. This exemplifies[36] a person with a noble character. It is a great example of how we should conduct ourselves in life.

People often deceive[37] others by telling lies to benefit themselves. Sometimes they even exhaust[38] themselves in spreading rumors[39] and creating trouble, all so that others are disadvantaged and fooled. But in the end, the lies we create will hurt us as well, because we damage the trust of others. We waste energy maintaining an illusion[40] that eventually becomes a burden because we know all along, it is a lie.

Buddhism speaks of the importance of not lying, for it is against the notion of truth and compassion. Lies not only create problems and sufferings for others

VOCABULARY

36. exemplifies (v.) 例證；例示
37. deceive (v.) 欺騙
38. exhaust (v.) 使筋疲力盡
39. rumors (n.) 謠言
40. illusion (n.) 幻覺；幻想

　　沒多久，皇帝就從大臣那裡聽說道楷禪師寧可受罰，也不說假話之事，大為讚歎欣賞，便將禪師釋放了。

but also for ourselves as we work to cover up one lie after another. We should learn to always be honest. When we are honest, our voices reflect confidence and certainty, and we naturally improve our ability to express our minds. Honesty shall enable us to speak our true minds, eliminating[41] any distracting[42] thoughts, and allowing us to concentrate[43] on delivering our messages of faith. Through honest communication, we improve our relationships with others; our attitude toward life will also prosper as we eliminate the harmful consequences[44] of lying.

VOCABULARY

41. eliminating (v.) 除去
42. distracting (adj.) 分散注意力的
43. concentrate (v.) 專注
44. consequences (n.) 結果；後果

在利益當頭，甚至攸關身命安危之際，道楷禪師寧可以自己吃虧，也不說假話，這是君子風範，實在是我們做人的典範。

Dharma Words by Venerable Master Hsing Yun

A word of truth is priceless;
it is a thousand times more precious than gold or silver.
Human virtue is priceless;
it is a thousand times taller than the highest mountain.

星雲大師法語

一句真理無價寶，比金比銀萬倍好；
人間道德無價寶，比山比嶽萬倍高。

notes

09

On Precept

Discipline

受 杖 自 責

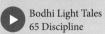
Bodhi Light Tales
65 Discipline

Once upon a time, during the Jin dynasty, there lived an eminent[1] monk named Master Dao'an, a great leader and teacher. Wishing to preserve[2] Buddhism, Master Dao'an sent his disciples to many different places to spread the Buddha's teachings. Among his many disciples, Fayu was especially talented and well-learned[3]. The relationship between the master and his disciple went beyond words, and Fayu often understood his teacher's teachings without the need for further explanation.

Eventually, Fayu was appointed[4] abbot of a monastery, and leader of a community of 400 people. He was respected and known for his strict monastic discipline[5]. Many people came to seek his teachings. However, there were times when some members of the monastery did not strictly follow the precepts as laid down by Fayu.

One day, after breakfast, one of his disciples said to him, "Abbot, there is a problem I am unsure whether to bring to your attention or not."

VOCABULARY

1. eminent (adj.) 顯赫的；有名的
2. preserve (v.) 維護；維持
3. well-learned (adj.) 學識淵博的
4. appointed (v.) 任命；委任
5. discipline (n.) 紀律；訓誡

　　東晉時代的法遇大師是一寺的住持，領導住眾數百人，平常規矩嚴謹，道風遠播十方，受到僧信的敬重。然而再清淨的僧團，龍蛇雜處，分子難免良莠不齊。

"If speaking up leads to the improvement[6] of our community, please go ahead," Abbot Fayu said.

"Yes, master. There have been rumors that one of our members has broken the precepts by getting drunk. It seems he's been out and about in town till late, drinking with townsfolk[7] and socializing[8] too much," the disciple reported.

The Abbot was silent for a while and then said, "I see… Please ask this disciple to come to see me."

Soon after, the disciple appeared and said, "Abbot, you asked for me?"

"Yes, please take a seat." Gesturing[9] for him to sit in front of him, the Abbot continued, "How long has it been since you renounced?"

"Nearly 10 years," the disciple replied.

"In your 10 years of practice, what can you share about the Five Precepts[10]?" the Abbot asked.

"First is refrain from killing; second, refrain from stealing; third, refrain from sexual

VOCABULARY

6. improvement (n.) 改進
7. townsfolk (n.) 鎮民；市民
8. socializing (v.) 參加社交活動；交際
9. gesturing (v.) 作手勢
10. Five Precepts (n.) 五戒

　　曾有一位徒眾，品行不端，和俗人混跡玩樂，甚至結伴喝酒。原本飲酒是犯根本大戒，應該處以遷單，逐出寺院，然而法遇大師顧念他是初犯，並沒有做出踰矩的行為，於是責罵一頓了事。

misconduct; fourth, refrain from lying; and fifth refrain from intoxicants," the disciple replied.

"You know the Five Precepts very well. Do you practice them diligently[11]?" Abbot asked.

"Well... I think that perhaps... maybe not..." the disciple muttered[12].

"Is it true that not long ago, you broke one of the precepts?" the Abbot asked with a firm[13] voice.

The disciple stayed still and quiet, and the Abbot continued, "As a monastic, you cannot forget your precepts and vows[14]. As monastics, we must guard our behavior and be conscious[15] at all times that we do not break the precepts we have taken. Guarding our body, speech, and mind is essential! If you choose to behave like a layperson, then you do not qualify to be a monastic. Do you understand?"

"Yes, master," the disciple replied softly.

"In observing strict monastic discipline, breaking the fifth precept, refraining from intoxicants, is considered a serious issue. Since

VOCABULARY

11. diligently (adv.) 勤奮地
12. muttered (v.) 喃喃低語
13. firm (adj.) 堅定的；嚴格的
14. vows (n.) 誓願
15. conscious (adj.) 有意識的；自覺的

事後，這件「飲酒事件」傳到法遇的老師道安大師的耳中，道安大師叫人送來一樣東西給法遇。法遇打開師父寄來的東西，一看是一個竹筒，裡面包了一根棍子，無隻字片語。他心知肚明，老師責備他課徒不嚴，執法不夠嚴峻。

this is your first mistake, I shall not expel you from the monastery. However, this is your final warning. Do you understand?" the Abbot said.

"Yes, master," the disciple replied.

Since that day, though lectured[16] by his master, the disciple, deep down, had no intention to change. He continued to sneak[17] out of the monastery to go into town.

His unruliness[18] and continued transgressions[19] soon reached the ears of Master Dao'an.

"Master, news has spread about Master Fayu's disciple. He broke his precept regarding taking intoxicants, often getting drunk. This disciple was once so hungover that he forgot to attend to his duties in the Main Shrine. As a rule, he should be expelled. Yet all Master Fayu did was scold[20] him. What are your thoughts on this?" one of Master Dao'an's disciples asked.

Master Dao'an thought for a while and replied, "Fetch me a cane and a hollow bamboo stick."

VOCABULARY

16. lectured (v.) 嚴責；訓斥
17. sneak (v.) 偷偷溜走
18. unruliness (n.) 無法無天；任性
19. transgressions (n.) 違反；犯罪
20. scold (v.) 責罵

他立即召集全山大眾，把師父寄來的竹筒供在佛前，燒香致敬；命維那行仗三下，垂淚自責。徒眾們看到法遇大師勇於承擔，接受老師杖棍的處分。從此戒規更加森嚴，而那位喝酒犯戒的徒眾也深感慚愧，不再攀緣俗務，專心用功修行。

The disciple did as he was told. Master Dao'an then carefully placed the cane inside the bamboo stick, and then on the outside he simply wrote, "To Fayu." He then instructed his disciple to send it right away.

Soon after, Fayu received the bamboo stick sent by his master. He unwrapped[21] it to find only a cane inside without a note or explanation.

Knowing exactly what his master meant, Fayu called everyone in the monastery to gather in the shrine. The shrine attendant lit the candles and incense as Fayu placed the cane on the altar in front of the Buddha. When everyone arrived, Fayu walked up to the altar[22] and prostrated[23] to the Buddha three times. He then addressed everyone, "As the leader of this monastery and teacher to you all, I have failed in my duty to guide you in observing strict monastic discipline. I deserve[24] to be punished." He then instructed the Disciplinarian[25] to hit him three times with the cane sent by Master Dao'an. Master Fayu's disciples sat in shock.

VOCABULARY

21. unwrapped (v.) 打開
22. altar (n.) 佛桌
23. prostrated (v.) 禮拜
24. deserve (v.) 應受；應得
25. Disciplinarian (n.) 糾察

　　身教重於言教，法遇大師雖貴為一寺的住持，卻能坦然受教老師的處分，當眾承擔杖棍的責罰。由於他勇於認錯，令徒眾更加心悅誠服，使得他能夠統理大眾，一切無礙。

Not only did they witness their master's sincere repentance[26], they also learned an invaluable[27] lesson in taking responsibility for one's actions.

Seeing his teacher's self-imposed[28] punishment, the disciple who had broken the fifth precept felt deep remorse[29] and vowed to never break any precept again. From that day on, everyone in the monastery practiced diligently and observed strict discipline.

This story highlights that teaching by example is more important than teaching by words. As teachers, parents, or leaders, we ought to teach and lead by example rather than through words. If one cannot walk the talk, why should anyone follow? If one leads by example, not only will they be respected, others will surely willingly follow them too.

Whenever one's students, children, or subordinates[30] refuse to learn and be taught, it is good for teachers and leaders to stop and reflect: Have my actions exemplified my words? Do my actions match what I have said? As the saying goes, "Actions speak louder than words."

身為老師、父母、主管，語言的教導比不上身教的力行，學生、孩子、屬下等不肯受教時，我們應該回頭省思自己的言行是否任意違背了自己所立的法規？

In this story, although Fayu was the abbot of the monastery, he bravely accepted Master Dao'an's punishment in front of everyone. His courage in admitting[31] and repenting his faults gained the respect of his disciples. Fayu knew he had failed as a teacher in guiding his disciples correctly. All were deeply moved, and respected him for being honest and taking responsibility for his actions. As a result, he was able to lead his community unhindered[32], peacefully, and in harmony.

VOCABULARY

31. admitting (v.) 承認
32. unhindered (adj.) 不受阻礙的

Dharma Words by Venerable Master Hsing Yun

A mediocre teacher lectures.
A good teacher explains.
An excellent teacher demonstrates.
A great teacher inspires.

星雲大師法語

平庸的老師，只會敘述。
良好的老師，懂得講解。
優異的老師，能夠示範。
偉大的老師，重在啟發。

notes

10

Two Wives

一妻一妾

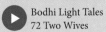
Bodhi Light Tales
72 Two Wives

Once upon a time in the nineteenth century, there lived a man named Harold. At that time, polygamy[1] was rather common. So, Harold had two wives, Josephine and Priscilla.

Josephine, a successful businesswoman, met Harold through work. Harold had always wanted many children. But, sadly, Josephine had fertility[2] issues that strained[3] their relationship. After long discussions, she agreed for Harold to marry a second time.

Priscilla was introduced to Harold through a friend. She was young and beautiful, with a sense of humor that Harold admired[4]. Both women had their strengths[5] and Harold loved them equally for who they were.

The three of them had an agreement. As Harold's first wife, Josephine had the right to make all decisions regarding the family. Priscilla, as the second wife, had to help with the house chores.

At first, as they were adjusting to this new lifestyle, family life was peaceful and

VOCABULARY

1. polygamy (n.) 一夫多妻；一妻多夫
2. fertility (n.) 生育能力
3. strained (v.) 使 (關係) 緊張；使承受壓力
4. admired (v.) 欽佩；仰慕
5. strengths (n.) 優點；長處

中國歷史上，不少男士坐享「齊人之福」，擁有一妻一妾，甚至一妻多妾。其實一個男人坐擁妻妾並不好，你疼愛一個，另外一個就不歡喜，只會讓自己左右為難、麻煩上身，無法獲得幸福美滿。

harmonious[6]. They got along well with each other.

One month after they all moved in together, it was Josephine's 35th birthday. Harold bought her a golden necklace to celebrate; but Priscilla became jealous[7] and said to Harold, "That's sweet. But I prefer a diamond necklace. Will you promise to get me one for my birthday?"

Before Harold could reply, Josephine said, "Priscilla, there's no need to talk about your birthday right now. It's MY birthday, so I deserve[8] the attention today!" Josephine grabbed[9] Harold's arm and continued, "Harold, remember our deal when you took a second wife. I only agreed if I could be in charge of all the decisions in this household."

"Yes, I remember our agreement," Harold replied.

Priscilla was very unhappy but decided not to push further as it was Josephine's birthday. From that day on, both wives would constantly[10] compete for Harold's attention. Over time,

VOCABULARY

6. harmonious (adj.) 和睦的
7. jealous (adj.) 妒忌的
8. deserve (v.) 應受；應得
9. grabbed (v.) 抓握
10. constantly (adv.) 不變地；不斷地

話說有一個男人討了兩個老婆，三人之間有一個規定：三人同床，妻子睡右邊，妾睡左邊，丈夫睡在中間。為了免得妻妾說他不公平，男人平時睡覺都不敢妄動一下。有一個夜晚，狂風暴雨襲來，導致屋頂漏水，

Harold thought, "If only they could see that I love them both equally. All I wish for is some peace and quiet in this house."

The rift[11] between Josephine and Priscilla worsened when Priscilla became pregnant[12]. One evening, Priscilla boasted[13] to Josephine, "When I give birth to my child, Harold will be thrilled[14], and he'll care more for me than you! How do you feel about that?"

Angry, Josephine replied, "That doesn't bother me at all! Even if you have a child, I'm still in charge. Remember, your child will have to obey me and follow my rules."

Priscilla cried out, "Harold... this is unfair! Why should she be in charge of MY children?!?"

"All right, stop arguing! I can't take this anymore!" Harold said with a firm voice.

Seeing how his two wives fought for his attention[15], he suggested, "To make sure you both equally receive my attention, from now on, the three of us will share the same bed. Josephine, you will sleep on my right, and

VOCABULARY

11. rift (n.) 裂痕
12. pregnant (adj.) 懷孕的
13. boasted (v.) 自誇
14. thrilled (v.) 震顫；激動
15. attention (n.) 關心

泥漿隨著雨水不斷地滲入屋內，恰好就滴在床鋪中間的位置。任憑泥漿怎樣滴到男人的眼睛裡，他還是不敢亂動，深怕朝左面看，妻子不歡喜；朝右面瞧，惹妾惱怒。最後，他的兩個眼睛就這樣瞎了。

Priscilla, you will sleep on my left. Is this fair enough?"

"Yes, I'm okay with this rule, but only if you don't toss and turn," Josephine replied.

"I guess if you're in the middle, then that's fair," Priscilla replied.

With this new arrangement[16], Josephine and Priscilla had fewer arguments in getting Harold's attention. Harold seemed to have found the peace and quiet he wished for.

One night, a violent storm brought torrential[17] rain. After three days of non-stop rain, the roof of the house began to leak. As the house was rather old and in need of repairs, mud began to seep[18] into the house along with the rain. Harold, sleeping in the middle, woke up in the middle of the night with his face drenched[19] in muddy[20] water. Feeling uncomfortable, he turned to his right, thinking to ask Josephine to help him. But his movement woke Priscilla. She whispered to him, "Why is Josephine getting your attention?"

VOCABULARY

16. arrangement (n.) 安排
17. torrential (adj.) 如急流的；傾瀉似的
18. seep (v.) 滲出；滲流
19. drenched (v.) 弄濕
20. muddy (adj.) 泥濘的；渾濁的

Harold turned to Priscilla and tried to explain, "The rain... and the mud..." But before he could finish, Josephine was now awake and said, "I thought you agreed not to toss and turn. Why are you now facing Priscilla and not me?"

Unable to make both Priscilla and Josephine happy, Harold had no choice but to keep sleeping on his back, meaning that the muddy water continued to drip into his eyes the whole night. This caused a severe infection[21]. With the risk of long-term damage to his vision, Harold underwent treatment[22].

It was only then that both Josephine and Priscilla realized their constant bickering[23] for Harold's attention had caused their husband's eye infection.

Feeling contrite, Josephine said, "Oh my dear husband, I'm so sorry. I should have tried to see things from your perspective[24]. I had no idea how difficult it was for you to keep both Priscilla and me happy."

"Yes, I was being so childish, demanding[25]

VOCABULARY

21. infection (n.) 感染
22. treatment (n.) 治療
23. bickering (v.) 鬥嘴
24. perspective (n.) 視角;觀點
25. demanding (v.) 要求

所以,一妻一妾,不是齊人之福,而是齊人之難。

在這個世間上,讓人左右兩難的事情所在多有。但是所謂的「求公平」,也並非是呆板的要求兩邊平衡。就像有時候你見到甲,邀請他到家裡坐坐,見到乙,不一定就要請他坐,也可以邀他來喝茶。或者,你見到甲,對他招呼說:「你好!」

the same attention from you all the time. Please forgive me," Priscilla said.

Embracing[26] both his wives, Harold said, "I love you both very much and I just wish for us to live in harmony and peace. If it means being blind for you both to stop bickering, I am willing to trade[27] my eyesight for it."

Both Josephine and Priscilla shook their heads and said, "No, please don't. Harold, we love you very much." Josephine then said to Priscilla, "I'm so sorry." They embraced each other and made peace.

This story highlights a dilemma[28] faced by many. Having two wives seemed like a blessing for Harold, but it created disharmony in his household.

Just like when you bump into a friend when shopping. You may invite them to your house for tea. But when you meet another friend, you may choose to go to a cafe with them instead. Sometimes, you greet a friend with "hello," but greet other friends with "good morning." This illustrates that we can be flexible[29] when we encounter identical situations with different people. There is no need to be rigid[30] when considering

VOCABULARY

26. embracing (v.) 擁抱
27. trade (v.) 交換
28. dilemma (n.) 進退兩難的局面
29. flexible (adj.) 靈活的
30. rigid (adj.) 刻板的；僵化的

見到乙，也可以換說：「你早！」不一定都要同樣的問候語。

做人處事，方便善巧才是智慧，而不是一昧墨守成規才叫做公平。比方說，你喜歡吃飯，我就準備飯請

how to be fair towards others.

True wisdom is to conduct ourselves and approach situations with skillful and expedient means. Being strictly bound by conventions[31] is not a true act of fairness. For example, if a friend enjoys eating rice and vegetables, then we would cook them a nice meal featuring rice and vegetables. But if another friend enjoys eating noodles, then we would be inclined[32] to cook them a bowl of noodles instead.

Everyone has their needs and strengths. We are all unique. Even animals have their differences. For example, cows and horses eat grass, but we cannot expect dogs and pigs to eat grass as well. Some animals are carnivores[33] and others omnivores[34], each has their diet.

We should not always seek to please everyone in everything we do, nor should we be reluctant[35] to change or be flexible. Every situation is different and we should act according to the causes and conditions of that particular situation, at that particular moment. Being flexible requires true wisdom and applying expedient means is true fairness.

VOCABULARY

31. conventions (n.) 習俗；慣例
32. inclined (v.) 傾向於
33. carnivores (n.) 肉食動物
34. omnivores (n.) 雜食動物
35. reluctant (adj.) 不情願的

你吃；他喜歡吃麵，我就煮麵請他吃，人人各有所需、各有所好，不一定都要一樣。就像牛馬吃草，總不能也要豬狗吃草，畢竟豬狗有豬狗的飲食，牛馬有牛馬的飲食，不應事事求同，食古而不化，固執而不知變通。懂得變通才是智慧，方便才是平等啊！

Dharma Words by Venerable Master Hsing Yun

To act according to causes and conditions means to act in the interests of others.
To act according to principles means to choose what is right and stick to it,
not just adhering to old rules.

星雲大師法語

「隨緣」是立場互易，隨順環境，但決非隨便行事，苟且偷安。
「不變」是擇善固執，一以貫之，但不是墨守成規，泥古不化。

notes

11

On Precept

Sandalwood

賣檀香

83 Sandalwood

Once upon a time, there lived a sandalwood merchant named Cody. He thought highly of his sandalwood and worked hard at promoting[1] it.

"Quality sandalwood for sale. Come in and have a look!" Cody said to the passerby.

"The sweet scent[2] of your sandalwood has filled the street," the passerby told him.

"Would you like to buy some?" Cody asked.

"No thanks, I can't afford[3] it!" the onlooker replied and walked away.

Still confident[4], Cody continued to promote it. Many people were attracted by the fragrance[5] of his sandalwood, but all would simply leave after learning of the price. After a week, Cody began to worry as he had not sold a single piece of sandalwood.

One morning, as Cody opened his shop, he was greeted by another merchant, "Hello there! I'm Roy, nice to meet you!"

"Hi, I'm Cody. How's it going?" Cody replied.

"Pretty good. It's nice weather today so I hope we sell a lot! Wow! Your sandalwood smells

VOCABULARY

1. promoting (v.) 推銷
2. scent (n.) 香味
3. afford (v.) 買得起
4. confident (adj.) 有信心的
5. fragrance (n.) 芬芳；香味

熱鬧的市集裡，有一個賣檀香的阿明努力地推銷檀香，可是來往的顧客卻都嫌貴，不肯花錢買他的檀香，這樣的景況維持了好幾天。後來他看到一個賣木炭的小販，才一天的時間就把木炭賣完了。阿明心裡很懊惱：我的檀香不及木炭嗎？怎麼他的木炭一天就賣完呢？

amazing[6]! Unlike my charcoal..." Roy said.

"Yes, it's high-quality sandalwood but I haven't sold any this week," Cody said disappointedly.

Their conversation was interrupted[7] by a customer, "Are you open yet? I'd like to get some charcoal."

Roy replied happily, "Yes!" as he served the customer, another showed up to buy his charcoal. By noon, Roy had sold out.

In disbelief[8], Cody thought, "How is this possible?"

He asked Roy, "Why is your charcoal selling better than my sandalwood?"

"Because charcoal is cheap and much needed by every household[9]. Everyone needs to cook, so they always need charcoal. Besides, my charcoal is priced fairly[10]. Anyway, good luck with your sandalwood. I'm off now!" Roy replied.

For the rest of the day, Cody still had no luck in selling his sandalwood. As he packed

VOCABULARY

6.   amazing (adj.) 令人驚詫的;令人驚喜的
7.   interrupted (v.) 中斷
8.   disbelief (n.) 不信;懷疑
9.   household (n.) 一戶;家庭
10. fairly (adv.) 公正地;公平地

他忍不住問賣木炭的小販:「你的木炭為什麼這麼好賣?」

小販細心地為他解說:「每戶人家煮飯燒菜都用得到木炭,而且我這個木炭是黑色的,更好賣!」

up his shop, he thought about what Roy said. An idea popped[11] into his head, "What if I sell my sandalwood for the same price as Roy's charcoal? Maybe I'll manage to sell it all too!"

The next day, feeling confident, Cody opened his shop. He began promoting the new price of his sandalwood. Soon, people began queuing[12] up to buy his sandalwood. Some even bought more than one piece!

One satisfied customer said to a passerby, "This sandalwood is on sale! It's as cheap as charcoal, get it while you can!"

Before noon, Cody had sold out.

Happily, he packed up and said to Roy, "Thanks for the tip[13]! You gave me the idea to lower my price. It's not even noon yet, but I've sold it all. Good luck with your charcoal, I'm off now." Cody waved Roy goodbye.

As Cody left, Roy smiled smugly[14], thinking how very foolish Cody was for selling such high-quality sandalwood at such a ridiculously[15] cheap price.

VOCABULARY

11. popped (v.) 突然出現
12. queuing (v.) 排隊
13. tip (n.) 指點；指導
14. smugly (adv.) 自鳴得意地
15. ridiculously (adv.) 荒謬地

阿明終於明白，黑色的才好賣。於是他將所有的檀香燒成黑色，再運到市集兜售，果然燒黑的檀香一下子就賣完了。

愚痴的阿明只想到要將檀香賣完，卻不知道木炭有木炭的價值，檀香有檀香的價值，把珍寶當做瓦礫來販賣，便宜賤賣，當然人人搶購。

This story highlights that the value and use of something depend on how we view and make use of it. In this story, Cody was too focused on[16] selling all of his sandalwood. He failed to see that sandalwood and charcoal each have their own value and use. Lowering the price of his sandalwood to match that of the charcoal is like selling gold for the price of copper. Though Cody managed to sell all of his sandalwood, would he have made enough of a profit to break even[17], or did he lose more than he actually gained?

Instead, Cody could have considered[18] another approach[19], such as selling his sandalwood at another market where customers were able and willing to pay his original price. If only he'd realized the true value of his sandalwood and how to make use of it, he would not have compared his sandalwood to Roy's charcoal.

In other words, if you know how to best make use of something, then it shall become valuable and precious. However, that same item given to someone who doesn't know how to make use of it, whether it be precious stones or pearls, would be a waste. In the same vein[20], if a person with the right talent is placed

VOCABULARY

16. focused on (pv.) 集中；特別關注
17. break even (v.) 收支平衡
18. considered (v.) 考慮；細想
19. approach (n.) 方式；方法
20. in the same vein (phr.) 同樣地

同樣的物品在會運用的人手上，是珍品；不會運用的人，珍珠瑪瑙也會變成廢土砂石。就如同一個人才，放對位置，則彼此獲益；不懂賞識，再優等的良馬也視作劣馬用來推磨子，不也枉然！世間萬物萬靈必定都有價值，但看明眼巧手如何提煉、抽絲剝繭！若是用人不當、用物不當、用言不當，不但錯失良機良緣良才，更造成浪費。

in the right position, it benefits everybody. However, if that same person is undermined[21], unappreciated[22], or placed in the wrong position, then no one benefits. Wouldn't that be a shame?

Everything in this world has value, but the best among us know how to use it, refine it, and make the most of it. It doesn't matter if it is people, objects, words, or even ourselves; if used improperly, then good opportunities will be missed, good causes and conditions will be wasted, and talents neglected[23]. Anything with potential would end in waste.

Therefore, we must learn to make the best use of everything around us, including talents. To know how to best make use of everything, we must first establish correct values, cultivate a broad vision, and think deeply about the pros[24] and cons[25]. In this way, we gain the ability and insight on how to best use everything around us.

VOCABULARY

21. undermined (v.) 使削弱信心
22. unappreciated (v.) 不受賞識
23. neglected (v.) 忽視；疏忽
24. pros (n.) 好處；益處
25. cons (n.) 不利條件；弊病

善於運用才人，首要建立正確的價值觀念，培養寬廣的視野，時時深入思考，才能具備識才識物，以及會用、懂得用的能力與見解，才不至於將珍貴的檀香燒黑，便宜賣了。

Dharma Words by Venerable Master Hsing Yun

Everything has its pros and cons, simply understand how to weigh them. Always keep sight of what is possible, for even dry stones and rotten wood can be used as medicine.

星雲大師法語

凡事皆有利弊，只要懂得權衡之道，

往大處著眼，枯石朽木也能入藥。

notes

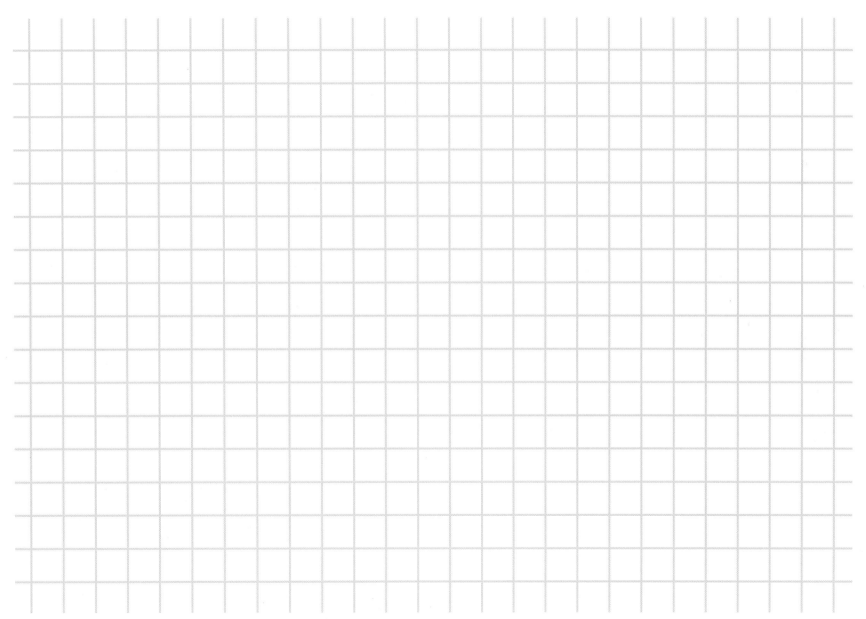

12

On Precept

Candy Craving

老人抓糖

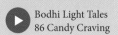
Bodhi Light Tales
86 Candy Craving

Once upon a time, there lived an old man named Desmond. He lived alone after his wife had passed away[1]. His two children, Grace and Leo, were married and lived in another city. On the weekends, Grace and Leo would take turns[2] visiting their father.

One Saturday, it was Leo's turn to visit. He arrived at the house and said, "Dad, I'm back! I got something for you."

Sitting in front of the TV, Desmond's eyes lit[3] up as he said, "Candy!"

"Yes! Mixed ones, too!" Leo replied.

Without waiting, Desmond took a piece of candy, put it in his mouth, and said, "Oh... this one is so good!" Before he'd even finished the first piece, he reached out for another, "This one looks yummy[4] too! I must try it."

Seeing how excited his father was, Leo said, "Dad, go easy on[5] them okay? They're all yours, there's no need to finish them all in one go."

"Do you remember when you were little? I once brought you a jar of candy from a business

VOCABULARY

1. passed away (pv.) 逝世
2. take turns (pv.) 輪流；依次
3. lit (v.) 發光
4. yummy (adj.) 美味的
5. go easy on (idiom) 對……有節制

在幽靜的鄉間住著一個老人，平時沒有什麼嗜好，就是喜歡吃糖。為此，居住在都市的兒孫，每逢假日一定會買點糖，回去孝養老人家。

trip[6] and you ate it all in one go?" Desmond said.

Leo laughed and said, "Yes, they were so nice I couldn't stop eating them."

"They vanished[7] so quickly that Grace never got a chance to eat any," Desmond replied.

"Yes! By the way, it's a long weekend next week, and Grace is busy. So how about we make a trip of it and you come to my place? Your grandson misses you," Leo said.

Desmond, still enjoying the candy, nodded in agreement[8].

On the following long weekend, Desmond arrived at Leo's place. After greeting everybody, Leo's son went up to Desmond and said, "Grandpa, this is for you."

Desmond took the jar, smiled, and said, "Thank you!"

After taking a seat in the living room, Desmond looked at the jar and exclaimed[9], "Wow! More candy! One big jar, too!" As he held up the jar and examined[10] the contents, he continued, "And there are so many new flavors."

VOCABULARY

6. business trip (n.) 出差
7. vanished (v.) 消失；不見
8. agreement (n.) 同意；答應
9. exclaimed (v.) 呼喊；驚叫
10. examined (v.) 仔細查看；檢查

有一次，老人到都市裡探望兒孫。兒孫心想：老父親難得來，應該多買一些糖給他吃。於是他們買回一大罐的糖果，正當老人將手伸進糖罐後，不知怎麼的，竟卡在裡頭出不來了。

"Yes, I drove past a candy shop the other day and saw this jar. I thought I would give it to you as a surprise," Leo said.

Pointing at a piece of candy, Desmond said, "I want to try this one!" He then quickly opened the jar and put his hand in it. As he tried to pull his hand out, he yelled, "Oh no... I'm stuck[11]!!"

Leo rushed[12] to help his father and tried to pull his hand, but Desmond yelled again, "No, stop! It hurts and it won't come free!"

"How about if I hold the jar and you try to pull your hand out yourself?" Leo suggested[13].

Desmond tried and cried, "No, I can't."

Seeing their struggle[14], Leo's wife said, "What if we break the jar?"

Moments later, she returned with a hammer[15] and handed it to Leo.

"All right, we just have to try it. Dad, please stay calm, okay?" Leo said.

兒孫聽到老人家求救的聲音，紛紛趕來幫忙，大家一陣忙亂，還是拔不出來，不得已只好把糖罐打破。糖罐破後，看見老人緊握著大把糖果的拳頭，終於恍然大悟，由於老人手裡抓了太多糖果，才會困在糖罐中，不得出離。

VOCABULARY

11. stuck (v.) 卡住
12. rushed (v.) 趕緊
13. suggested (v.) 建議
14. struggle (n.) 掙扎
15. hammer (n.) 槌

Desmond nodded.

Leo gently smashed the jar with the hammer, shattering[16] it into pieces. Candies fell everywhere and everyone's jaws dropped. What they saw was Desmond's hand clenched[17] in a fist, holding tight onto a single piece of candy. It was then that Leo realized why his father's hand was stuck.

"Finally!" Desmond said and smiled as he popped the candy into his mouth.

This story teaches us that when a person is overly greedy, trouble awaits. In this story, Desmond's greed for more candy is a good reminder for us. When we see something we like, should we also grasp[18] for more? Or are we aware of our greed?

For example, if one craves wealth, they will do whatever is necessary to get it. If one craves love, they will suffer all kinds of grievances[19]. Moreover, one must endure much torment[20] for the sake of wealth and fame. In the end, they will all be overwhelmed

VOCABULARY

16. shattering (v.) 粉碎
17. clenched (v.) 緊握
18. grasp (v.) 抓
19. grievances (n.) 委屈；苦境
20. torment (n.) 苦痛

一個人過分貪心，麻煩就多。為了想發財，費盡多少辛勞；為了情愛，受盡種種委屈；為了貪圖功名富貴，不知受了多少苦刑……不知滿足，注定終身貧窮，誠如《須賴經》所說：「財業雖豐廣，而不知充飽，大海尚可滿，是貧終不足。」

with dissatisfaction and bound to lead a miserable[21] life. Just as said in a Buddhist sutra, "Though there is boundless wealth, without a sense of fulfillment and contentment[22], one would still feel empty and unhappy even if they own an ocean of wealth."

Life's greatest treasure is contentment. A contented person, though they may sleep on the floor, would still feel like they were in heaven. A discontented person, though in heaven, would still feel like they were in hell.

Most people seek wealth and fame from without.

All day long they rush about and keep themselves busy, just for the sake[23] of filling a bottomless pit[24]. As the saying goes, "You may own a mansion with a thousand rooms, but you can only sleep on a six-foot bed at once; You may own ten thousand acres of land, but all you need is a bowl of rice per meal." True wealth lies not in our material possessions[25] and external gains but in the contentment that we cultivate within.

The Poet Master Hanshan wrote, "I rest where I please in the Three Realms, idle, with nothing to do.

VOCABULARY

21. miserable (adj.) 痛苦的；悲慘的
22. contentment (n.) 滿足；知足
23. sake (n.) 為了
24. bottomless pit (n.) 無底洞；無休止的情形
25. possessions (n.) 財產

人生最寶貴者，便是「知足」。知足的人，雖臥地上猶如天堂；不知足的人，雖在天堂也如同地獄。

大部分的人，多由心外求富貴，終日奔波，只為填滿那一口無底洞，然而「大廈千間，夜眠不過八尺；良田萬頃，日食又能幾何？」真正的富貴不在心外的擁

The bright moonlight and the clear breeze: these are my home." This saying implies[26] that a bright moon and a clear breeze are enough to satisfy a person like Master Hanshan. If one has joy, compassion, humility[27], and gratitude[28] within, then why is there the need to seek wealth and fame without?

有，而在內心的滿足。寒山大師不也說：「三界橫眠閒無事，明月清風是我家。」我心中有歡喜、有慈悲、有慚愧、有感恩，又何必心外求富貴。一輪明月，一襲清風，便足以讓人覺得滿足了。

Dharma Words by Venerable Master Hsing Yun

Greed, anger, and ignorance are the worst sufferings in the world;
Loving-kindness, compassion, joy, and generosity
are the best wealth in the world.

星雲大師法語

貪瞋愚昧，人間至苦；
慈悲喜捨，人間至富。

13

On Precept

The Human-Faced Ulcer

人面瘡的故事

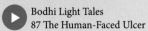
Bodhi Light Tales
87 The Human-Faced Ulcer

Human bodies can develop many different diseases such as ulcers[1] and sores[2]. Once upon a time, there was a story about a particular kind of ulcer that had a human face, complete with eyes, nose, and a mouth that meant this ulcer also needed to be fed. This story of the Human-Faced Ulcer is said to have happened to Chan Master Zhi Xuan, who later on in the Tang dynasty became the renowned National Master Wu Da.

Once upon a time, Master Zhi Xuan was on a study trip. On his journey, he met another monastic who had ulcers all over his body and smelled[3] so bad nobody wanted to be near him. Master Zhi Xuan felt sorry for the monastic and decided to care for him until he recovered[4]. When the monastic had recovered, he said to Master Zhi Xuan, "Thank you so much for taking care of me. If you ever find yourself in any trouble[5], please come look for me at Jiulong Mountain in Sichuan. When you can see the twin pine trees, you will have arrived at my place."

VOCABULARY

1. ulcers (n.) 潰瘍
2. sores (n.) 瘡
3. smelled (v.) 發出……氣味
4. recovered (v.) 痊癒
5. trouble (n.) 困難；麻煩

　　人的身體有很多疾病，其中有一種瘡疾，叫做「人面瘡」，是長在人的膝蓋上，形相如人一般，五官齊全，還有一張口，每天也要吃飯。這則「人面瘡」的故事，是發生在唐朝知玄悟達國師的身上。

"All right, I will keep that in mind. Thank you," replied Master Zhi Xuan.

Actually, without realizing it, Master Zhi Xuan had just helped an enlightened being named Kanaka.

Years later, Master Zhi Xuan's virtuous[6] conduct won him the praise and respect of Emperor Yizong. He was given the honorable title of "National Master Wu Da," meaning "the thoroughly enlightened one." Furthermore, the Emperor granted him a precious throne made of sandalwood. After receiving this throne, National Master Wu Da unknowingly gave rise to thoughts of arrogance[7] and vanity[8]. Over time, a huge ulcer began to grow on one of his knees, with all the features of a human face. This "Human-Faced Ulcer" caused the National Master unbearable[9] pain. However, he did not cry out or complain, as he knew deep down that this resulted from his karmic retribution[10].

VOCABULARY

6. virtuous (adj.) 道德高尚的；擁有美德的

7. arrogance (n.) 自大

8. vanity (n.) 虛榮心

9. unbearable (adj.) 無法忍受的

10. karmic retribution (n.) 業報；業果

　　唐朝的知玄禪師有一次外出雲遊參學，半路遇到一位同道。這位同道的身上長了瘡，並且發出惡臭，沒有人敢和他往來。知玄禪師心生憐憫，便主動給予照料，直到他身體康復為止。同道心中非常感謝，就對禪師說：「將來如果你有什麼苦難，可以到四川彭州九隴山來找我。只要看到二棵大松樹並連在一起，就是我居住的地方了。」其實，這位同道是個阿羅漢，名叫迦諾迦尊者。

One day, as the pain became extremely[11] unbearable, he suddenly remembered what Kanaka had said to him years ago. So, he decided to seek[12] help and headed to Jiulong Mountain.

When the National Master arrived at Kanaka's place, it was already evening, and so he was offered a place to stay for the night. The next day, Kanaka's attendant[13] came to him, "Good morning National Master Wu Da, I hope you slept well."

"Yes, I did. Thank you," replied the National Master.

"Master Kanaka has asked me to take you to the spring[14] where you can wash the ulcer on your knee," the attendant said.

"Yes. Thank you so much."

After arriving at the spring, feeling hot and in excruciating[15] pain, the National Master sat down next to the water. He then began to wash his knee. Suddenly, the ulcer began to speak

---

VOCABULARY

11. extremely (adv.) 非常地；極度地

12. seek (v.) 請求；尋求

13. attendant (n.) 侍者

14. spring (n.) 泉

15. excruciating (adj.) 劇烈疼痛的；極痛苦的

後來，知玄禪師因為道高德重，受到唐懿宗的恭敬，禮拜為師，並且敕封為「悟達國師」。坐上了皇帝賜予的檀香寶座，悟達國師可說備受禮遇，不知不覺就生起了虛榮心。不久，他發現膝上害了人面瘡。國師深知這必定是因為自己的得失心，而招感業障現前，他想起過去那位同道臨別的叮囑，於是忍著痛苦，來到四川彭州九隴山。

to him, "National Master Wu Da, please stop. I must tell you something."

In disbelief[16], the National Master stopped and mumbled[17], "Are you talking to me?"

"Yes," the ulcer replied.

The National Master kept silent and looked at his knee.

The ulcer continued, "Do you know that we have met before? It was during the West Han dynasty. At that time, you were called Yuan Ang and I was Chao Cuo. But back then, you wronged me. You framed[18] me and the Emperor gave the order to have me killed. I suffered a horrific[19] death and I swore I would get revenge[20]. However, in your other past lives, you had always been a most honorable and virtuous monastic, always

VOCABULARY

16. disbelief (n.) 不信；懷疑
17. mumbled (v.) 含糊地說
18. framed (v.) 陷害
19. horrific (adj.) 極其可怕的
20. revenge (n.) 報仇

在同道的招呼下，悟達國師先是住了一宿。隔天，在一位童子帶領下，來到一處泉水邊。身上發熱、痛苦難耐的國師，掬起水來就要清洗人面瘡，但是瞬間，人面瘡竟然開口說話了，他說：「悟達國師，暫且不要清洗！我要告訴你，你我在西漢時代結下了冤仇，那時候你是袁盎，我是晁錯，因被你誣陷，招來殺身之禍，久已想要報仇雪恨。但由於十世以來，你都是一名高僧，所以我始終沒有辦法靠近你。到了這一世，因為你受到皇帝的恩寵，起了虛榮心，於福德有損，我才得

strict in observing the precepts. Therefore, I was unable to do anything to harm you. But in your present life, upon receiving the Emperor's praise, your vanity finally gave me my chance to get my revenge. Today, right here and now, with the purity of this water blessed by the enlightened Kanaka, I wish to let you know that the feud[21] between us is resolved[22], and the bad blood finally ended. I will no longer seek my revenge upon you."

On hearing this, the National Master was in shock, and he quickly splashed the ulcer with the spring water. The pain was so severe that he fainted. When he finally woke up, the ulcer had disappeared.

Because of this experience, National Master Wu Da wrote the *Compassionate Samadhi Water Repentance*, a text establishing how one can repent their transgression[23], and eliminate calamity[24] as well as karmic hindrances[25].

---

21. feud (n.) 長期爭鬥
22. resolved (v.) 解決；消除
23. transgression (n.) 過犯
24. calamity (n.) 災難
25. hindrances (n.) 障礙

以乘虛而入。今日承蒙迦諾迦尊者出面為你我解除冤業，賜給我三昧法水，令我得到清涼解脫，我們之間的宿怨，從此就一筆勾銷了。」

悟達國師聽了不覺心驚，連忙以清水洗淨人面瘡，痛徹肝腸，立刻讓他昏厥了過去。奇妙的是，等到他甦醒過來，人面瘡也消失了。

由此因緣，後來悟達國師作了《慈悲三昧水懺》，敘說懺悔認錯可以消災免難。

This story shows us the importance of repentance. When our clothes become dirty, we can wash them clean with water. When our bodies become dirty, we can also wash them clean with water. When a person commits unwholesome[26] deeds, if they can repent sincerely, be willing to change, and show earnest remorse and humility[27], they will be able to atone[28] for their transgressions.

26. unwholesome (adj.) 不善的
27. humility (n.) 謙遜
28. atone (v.) 贖罪；彌補

　　從這一則故事中，我們可以知道懺悔的重要。衣服髒了，用水洗一洗就會乾淨；身體髒了，用水洗一洗，就會清潔；一個人縱然有一些罪業，只要誠心懺悔、肯得改過，懺悔的法水就能滅罪消愆。

Dharma Words by Venerable Master Hsing Yun

Repentance, like clear water, can cleanse the three unwholesome karmas;
Repentance, like clothing, can make our body, mind, and virtue august.

星雲大師法語

懺悔就像清水一樣，可以洗淨我們的三業罪障；
懺悔就像衣服一樣，可以莊嚴我們的身心功德。

14

A Lie Becomes Truth

謊言變真理

Bodhi Light Tales
96 A Lie Becomes Truth

Once upon a time, there lived a mother and her son, Nora, and Miles. Nora owned an embroidery[1] business and Miles worked as her sales rep[2]. Nora's embroidery was well-known in their community[3].

One day, Nora was working at home. Suddenly, her neighbor came over and said, "Oh Nora, I've just heard terrible[4] news! Miles has killed someone on West Street."

Nora looked up from her embroidery and replied, "Nonsense! My son would never kill anyone!" Without saying anything more, she calmly returned to her weaving[5].

Not long after, another neighbor came by and said, "Nora! Bad news! Your son killed someone!"

This time, Nora stopped her weaving and thought, "Could it be true? I don't think so..." She waved her hand and replied, "No way! Why would Miles kill someone? You must be

VOCABULARY

1. embroidery (n.) 刺繡
2. sales rep (n.) 銷售代表;推銷員
3. community (n.) 社區;群體
4. terrible (adj.) 可怕的;可怖的
5. weaving (v.) 編織

過去有人說,說謊超過三十次以上,謊言也成真理。

曾經,曾子的母親正在織布,忽然有一個鄰居匆匆跑來,說:「不得了!不得了!妳的兒子曾參在東街殺了人!」

曾母一聽,就說:「不會啦!我的兒子不會殺人啦!」她一點都不動心,還是很鎮定地繼續紡紗織布。

talking about someone else!" Still believing that her son would not kill anyone, Nora returned to her weaving.

Two hours later, one of her friends came to the house and said, "Something really bad has happened. Miles killed someone on the West Street!" Now feeling uneasy, Nora stopped her weaving and said, "Is this true?" Her friend nodded.

In a panic[6], Nora grabbed[7] her purse[8] and rushed to West Street. When she got to the crime scene[9], Miles was nowhere to be found. After asking the police officers in charge, she found out that the killer was someone also called Miles, but it was not her son.

Greatly relieved[10], Nora returned home.

VOCABULARY

6. panic (n.) 恐慌；驚惶
7. grabbed (v.) 攫取；抓取
8. purse (n.) 錢包
9. crime scene (n.) 犯罪現場
10. relieved (v.) 鬆了口氣

過了一會兒，又有一個人急急忙忙地趕來，說：「糟了啊！妳的兒子殺人了！」這回，曾母聽了以後，心裡就想：會這樣嗎？但她還是說：「不會啦！我的兒子怎麼會殺人？你說的恐怕是別人吧！」曾母仍然相信兒子不會殺人，安心地織著布。

This story highlights how dangerous rumors can be. Even the trust implicit[11] in the relationship between mother and son can be put to the test with a simple rumor. There is even a saying that a lie repeated thirty times becomes true. In this story, Nora was at first unmoved by the rumors regarding her son. However, when she heard that her son had killed someone for the third time, doubt began to set in her mind. There is another saying, "If you throw enough mud, some will stick." In other words, too many rumors can sow confusion[12] over what is right and wrong, true or false. Sadly, in today's world, such rumors disguised[13] as factual news are commonplace.

Someone once told the following story:

During a war, planes were sent to attack with bombs. Once the alert[14] of imminent[15] danger was sent out, someone would ask, "How many planes are coming?" Another person would answer, "Nine planes." As radio communications at that time were difficult, the message passed on and turned into "Nineteen

再過了一會兒,一個人急忙奔馳而來,說:「不得了啊!妳的兒子在東街殺了人!」曾母一聽,趕緊停下織布機,口中念道:「真是這樣嗎?」立刻就往事發現場奔跑而去。一探之下,才知道殺人者是另外一個也叫曾參的人,並不是她的兒子。

可見得即使親如母子,就像那麼信賴兒子賢能的曾母,經過了三個人的奔走相告,也會相信謊言可能是真的。所謂「眾口鑠金」,社會上很多消息的傳播,就是這樣而來的。

planes." As the message was passed along to a third person, the next number became "Ninety planes."

With only three people involved, the message was misheard twice, and the total number of planes became completely distorted[16]. This is how misleading[17] and dangerous a simple rumor can be.

We must always remember that virtuous people will write, speak, and conduct themselves with dignity[18] and honesty. If our society lacks morality[19] and virtue, it would be like the story of Nora and Miles, rumors would spread endlessly.

There is another saying, "A good deed goes unnoticed, but scandal[20] spreads fast."

Every day, there are people in society who do good deeds, but no one is seemingly interested as it is often rarely reported. However, when someone makes a mistake, it is often front-page news and widely reported. Bad situations are made worse, making people

VOCABULARY

16. distorted (adj.) 歪曲的；曲解的
17. misleading (adj.) 誤導的
18. dignity (n.) 尊嚴
19. morality (n.) 道德
20. scandal (n.) 醜聞

過去蔣經國先生說了一段故事。抗戰期間，日本人派遣飛機來轟炸，一拉警報之後，就有一個人問：「有多少架飛機？」有人回答：「是一架飛機。」聽的人沒聽清楚，聽成「十一架飛機」，所以，一架飛機就變成了十一架飛機。再有人問：「有多少架飛機？」他就轉告說：「就是十一架飛機啊！」然後，又有人問：「多少架飛機？」輾轉聽到消息的人就回答：「九十一架飛機。」

才只是三個人的消息傳播，飛機就從一架變成了九十一架，可見謠言的可怕。因此，一個有德的君

fearful[21] and anxious[22]. In looking after ourselves as well as society, we must take responsibility[23] for not spreading false and hurtful rumors. We must cultivate the practice of distinguishing[24] between right and wrong. It is only by working together that we can create a harmonious[25] world.

VOCABULARY

21. fearful (adj.) 害怕的
22. anxious (adj.) 焦慮的；焦急的
23. responsibility (n.) 責任
24. distinguishing (v.) 辨認；分辨
25. harmonious (adj.) 和諧的

子，寫文章，筆下要有德；講話，口中要有德。社會沒有了道德，就像「曾子殺人」的傳說，許多不實的傳聞就會紛至沓來。

所謂「好事不出門，壞事傳千里」，有時候，社會上的人做了一些好事，即便宣揚了，人家也不聽，覺得沒有趣味；反而做錯了一點無關緊要的事，就被渲染得極為嚴重，造成人心惶惶。為了愛護我們的社會、愛護我們自己，希望大家不要渲染事情，共同創造一個美好的世界，這才是我們的責任。

Dharma Words by Venerable Master Hsing Yun

To urge others to be good, you must first be upright yourself;
That is, "Do what I do" is better than "Do what I say."
To dispute rumors, you must first be upstanding;
That is, "Facts speak louder than words."

星雲大師法語

要勸化別人，首須端正自己，此乃「身教勝於言教」；
要辯解譏毀，先要健全自己，所謂「事實勝於雄辯」。

notes

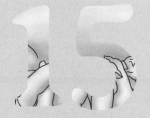

15

This Little Piggy

十一頭小豬

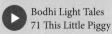

Bodhi Light Tales
71 This Little Piggy

Once upon a time, there lived a couple, Don and Sandra, who owned a butcher shop in a small town. Sandra had recently[1] given birth to a baby girl, named Ashley. Don ran the butcher shop alone while Sandra stayed home to look after the baby.

Each morning, a nearby monastery[2] would sound a gong to wake everyone in the monastery. Living close by, Don could hear the gong every morning. Eventually, the sound of the morning gong[3] became Don's alarm clock.

Once he heard the gong, he knew it was time to get up and get ready for work.

Don's routine[4] each morning was to slaughter[5] and prepare a single pig. Usually, by the time he finished, the morning sun would already be shining up high. It was the perfect time to bring the pork meat to the market as everyone would already be up and headed to the market for their daily shopping.

One afternoon, Don came home earlier as he'd sold everything. Pleased to see Don home

VOCABULARY

1. recently (adv.) 最近；近來
2. monastery (n.) 寺院
3. gong (n.) 鐘
4. routine (n.) 慣例
5. slaughter (v.) 屠宰；宰殺

張姓屠夫每天都要殺一頭豬供應鄉民的需要，以此維持自己的生活，這個殺豬的行業，一做就幾十年。屠夫張也曾經想過，殺生罪業很重，但由於自忖沒有別的長處，找不到其他謀生的門路，就這麼一天過一天。

early, Sandra said, "You're home early! How about we eat out tonight?"

"Yes! It's been a while, we have not eaten out since Ashley was born," Don replied.

"Speaking of Ashley, I noticed[6] something rather strange[7]. Each morning, right after the gong sounds, she won't stop crying. I've tried everything, feeding her, changing her nappy[8], but nothing worked."

"That is strange... Is it the gong that's bothering[9] her?" Don replied.

"That's what I first thought as well, but when the gong rings she still seemed all right. It's more obvious[10] when the gong stops ringing," Sandra said.

"I see... Well after the gong, I am busy preparing the meat for the market. But, I'll try to help you with her," Don replied.

"It's okay. Getting to the market early is important. I'll just bring it up at the next mother's group meeting, and see if anyone has any suggestions," Sandra said.

VOCABULARY

6. noticed (v.) 注意到；感覺到
7. strange (adj.) 奇怪的
8. nappy (n.) 尿布
9. bothering (v.) 煩擾；打擾
10. obvious (adj.) 明顯的

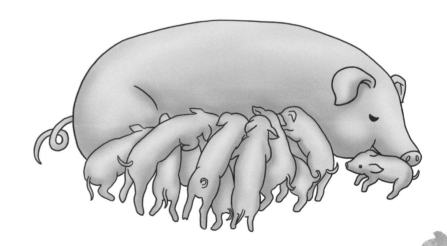

"All right," Don replied.

That evening, Don and Sandra had a nice dinner. When they got back home, Don prepared his tools[11] for the next morning, and then went to bed.

The next day, when Don woke up, it was already bright and sunny. He thought, "Oh no! I've overslept[12]! But... the gong... how come I didn't hear it?"

He looked over to Sandra who was still sound asleep, and Ashley was up but not crying, just babbling[13]. He got up and picked up Ashley. She smiled in his arms and Don thought, "This is the first time she smiles at me, usually, she's either crying or cranky[14] when I hold her." Sandra woke up and seeing Don with Ashley, smiled, and said, "Good morning!"

Don explained to her how he missed the morning gong and he might as well take the day off[15] now. Sandra agreed.

However, all morning, Don couldn't stop thinking about why the morning gong did not

VOCABULARY

11. tools (n.) 工具
12. overslept (v.) 睡過頭
13. babbling (v.) 牙牙學語
14. cranky (adj.) 壞脾氣的；易怒的
15. day off (n.) 休息日

屠夫張每天殺豬的時間，恰恰與都市不遠處寺廟早課的鐘聲同時，每日聽到鐘響他就起床，待殺完豬天色已大亮，村裡的人也準備上市場買菜，正是把豬擔出去叫賣的好時機。

sound. By lunchtime, Sandra suggested to Don that he go find out why as the mystery[16] was bothering him.

When Don arrived at the monastery, he was greeted by a monastic[17]. Don joined his palms and said, "Hello! My name is Don, I live just down the road."

"Nice to meet you, Don. What brings you here today?" the monastic said.

Don explained, "I usually hear the gong every morning. But this morning, I didn't hear it. I was just wondering why today, was there a particular reason?"

"Yes, you are right. Sounding the gong is a daily ritual[18] at our monastery. However, last night I had a dream. There were eleven piglets, all of them kneeling before me. One piglet had black spots[19] on his back. It came up to me and begged[20] me to save them all. I could not make sense of it. Each piglet told me that as long as I didn't ring the gong in the morning, they would all be saved. Then I woke up. This dream felt so

VOCABULARY

16. mystery (n.) 謎
17. monastic (n.) 出家人
18. ritual (n.) 儀式
19. spots (n.) 斑點;圓點
20. begged (v.) 乞求

有一晚,他將隔天要殺一隻母豬的工具都準備妥當,奇怪的是,隔天清晨一直沒有聽到寺院鐘聲。按捺不住心裡的疑惑,就到寺廟去詢問。年老的住持告訴他:「今天早上沒有叩鐘,是因為昨天夜裡,作了一個夢,夢見十一個小孩,跪到我的面前央求我救他們一命。他們告訴我,只要我明天早上不要叩鐘,他們就得救了,為了能救十一個小孩的寶貴生命,今天早上我就不叩鐘了。」

real. If you had seen their faces, you would know what I mean. I did not want to take the risk, I could not bear[21] to see the piglets suffer if the dream was true. So, this morning, I decided to skip the morning gong signal and bowed to the Buddha for forgiveness[22]," the monastic said.

"I see. Thank you for your time. I should probably head home now," Don replied.

On his way home, he thought about the conversation he had with the monastic. Then, a thought suddenly burst[23] into his mind, "A mother pig... Could it be...?" He rushed[24] home.

As soon as he reached the yard, he looked on in utter[25] shock. The pig that was meant to be slaughtered and prepared that very morning had given birth to piglets. Even more shocking to Don, he counted eleven little piglets in total. One of the piglets, with black spots on

屠夫張忽然有所感：「十一個小孩難道是母豬的孩子嗎？」

他趕回家中，果然今天早上逃過一命的母豬，剛剛生下小豬，算一算真是十一頭小豬。他感嘆輪迴轉世，因果絲毫不差，於是痛下決心，不再以殺豬為業。

VOCABULARY

21. bear (v.) 忍受
22. forgiveness (n.) 原諒；寬恕
23. burst (v.) 忽然出現；閃過
24. rushed (v.) 衝；奔
25. utter (adj.) 完全的；極度的

his back, came up and nudged[26] him. He knelt to pick up the piglet and when their eyes met, his heart melted[27]. He now knew exactly what the monastic meant. He too could not bear to see the piglets suffer. At that moment, Sandra walked in holding their baby girl. Seeing both families made whole, Don knew that he no longer wanted to be a butcher.

This story highlights how an act of compassion can have a great impact[28] on others, and can even save a life. The monastic sensed the suffering of the piglets and, out of compassion, fulfilled their request of not ringing the gong in the morning. This was not only an act of compassion but also a demonstration of expedient means. In Buddhism, bodhisattvas are often said to use expedient means, meaning they apply suitable and practical skills tailored[29] to help sentient beings according to their disposition[30].

The monastic's act of compassion ultimately changed the lives of the eleven piglets. Moreover, Don came to realize the cruelty of slaughtering animals. If the monastic had stuck to a strict rule that must

VOCABULARY

26. nudged (v.) 輕推；輕觸
27. melted (v.) 融化；熔化
28. impact (n.) 巨大影響；強大作用
29. tailored (v.) 特製
30. disposition (n.) 性格

老住持的方便應緣，救了母豬與十一隻小豬的生命，屠夫張也在老和尚的慈悲感化下，終於決定改行，從此免除刀下無辜的冤魂，也不再積累殺業。如果老住持堅持每天早上一定要叩鐘，那麼故事的結局必定完全改觀。

always be followed, in this case sounding the gong that morning, the outcome for the little piglets would have been far different. Instead, the monastic's kind thoughts also influenced[31] Don's actions and led him to change his lifestyle.

The actions of both the monastic and Don illustrate their ability to adapt according to the situation at hand. When adapting with kindness and compassion, the resulting effects are immeasurable[32]. A wise person who adapts[33] to circumstances[34] is like water that shapes itself into the vessel that holds it.

Learning to adapt requires acceptance[35] of any given situation. Following acceptance, we can then determine a way forward.

VOCABULARY

31. influenced (v.) 影響
32. immeasurable (adj.) 無限的
33. adapts (v.) 適應
34. circumstances (n.) 情況；情形
35. acceptance (n.) 接受

佛陀應病予藥，應機施教，是向我們示現方便法門，如果能有與人為善的方便，不輕易拒人於千里之外，這一點善念善行，勝造七層佛塔的功德。

Dharma Words by Venerable Master Hsing Yun

You do not have to believe in the Buddha,
but you must believe in the law of causality.
You can do without Buddhism,
but you can never do without compassion.

星雲大師法語

可以不信佛祖，但不能不信因果。
可以不信佛教，但不能沒有慈悲。

notes

notes

notes

Credits 致謝

The Bodhi Light Tales were initially published on the Bodhi Light Tales Anchor podcast channel. We would like to express our heartfelt gratitude to everyone for their dedicated efforts.

《星雲說喻》最初以英文有聲書形式於 Anchor 播客平台推出，為「菩提心燈」系列故事。今結集成冊，特此感謝製作團隊的付出。

Editor-in-Chief 主編:
Venerable Miao Guang 妙光法師

Project Manager 專案執行:
Venerable Zhi Sheng 知笙法師

English Translators 英文翻譯:
Venerable Zhi Sheng 知笙法師
Belinda Hsueh 薛瑋瑩
Angela Ho 何慧玲

English Editors 英文編輯:
Arthur van Sevendonck
Jennifer Hsu 許嫡娟
Neil Lee
Jenny Liu

Vocabulary Assistants 中英詞彙表整理:
Kathryn Lee 李苑嬝
Belinda Hsueh 薛瑋瑩
Handayani Fu

English Story Proofreaders 英文故事校稿:
Venerable Zhi Mu 知睦法師
Arthur van Sevendonck
Tom Halbert
Huang Hsin-yu 黃馨玉
Kathryn Lee 李苑嬝

Logo & Graphic Designer 平面設計:
Sedona Garcia

Illustrators (In order of illustrations contributed)
繪圖 (按圖次序):
Venerable Dao Pu 道璞法師
Venerable Neng Hui 能輝法師
Jack Yu 游智光
Lo Wan-ching 羅婉菁
Jonathon Cheung
Shi Jinhui 施金輝
Sedona Garcia
Venerable Zhi Yue 知悅法師
Zeng Jing-yi 曾靜怡
Valerie Tan

Podcast Audio Narrator 故事朗讀:
Venerable Miao Guang 妙光法師

Social Media Strategist 社群媒體策略:
Selene Chew 周思蕾

Podcast Intro & Outro Music Composer 音樂創作:
Nicholas Ng

Podcast Audio Editor 音檔剪輯:
Venerable Zhi Sheng 知笙法師

財團法人佛光山人間佛教研究院
Fo Guang Shan Institute of Humanistic Buddhism